DECOLONIZING
THEOLOGY

DECOLONIZING
THEOLOGY
A Caribbean Perspective

Noel Leo Erskine

ORBIS BOOKS
Maryknoll, New York 10545

The Catholic Foreign Mission Society of America (Maryknoll) recruits and trains people for overseas missionary service. Through Orbis Books Maryknoll aims to foster the international dialogue that is essential to mission. The books published, however, reflect the opinions of their authors and are not meant to represent the official position of the society.

"Black Theology and the Black Church" first appeared in *Theology Today* July 1979. "Christian Hope and Freedom in History" first appeared in *Hope for the Church* edited by Theodore Runyon. Copyright © 1979 by Abingdon. Used by permission.

Copyright © 1981 Orbis Books, Maryknoll NY 10545

Manufactured in the United States of America

Library of Congress Cataloging in Publication Data

Erskine, Noel Leo.
　Decolonizing theology.

　Includes bibliographical references and index.
　1. Black theology. 2. Liberation theology.
3. Caribbean area—Religion. I. Title.
BT82.7.E77　　230'.08996　　80-21784
ISBN 0-88344-087-3 (pbk.)

To Glenda

Contents

Preface

The Search for Freedom had its genesis some years ago in a sabbatical at Duke University. It was further developed while I was at Union Theological Seminary under the guidance of my friend and teacher, Professor James Cone.

While I thank James Cone for much wise counsel, I must take responsibility for the final product. I also thank my friend and colleague Theodore Runyon for reading much of this manuscript. Special thanks must be accorded to Janet Gary, who often gave beyond the call of duty in getting this manuscript ready.

Now that this work has reached its final stage, I would like to note that it has been a labor of love. But it has taken many long hours and my family has faithfully borne with me to the end. Their sacrifice shall always be remembered.

Introduction

I wish I knew how it would feel to be free,
I wish I could break all these chains holding me.
I wish I could say all the things I should say—
Say 'em loud, say 'em clear, for the whole world to hear.
                          —From the Harlem Renaissance

The longing for freedom to which these lines point is the central theme binding all oppressed peoples together. Whether one listens to the cry that resounds from the oppressed in Africa, the Caribbean, Latin America, Asia, or North America, this longing for freedom is expressed as the central theme of their theologies.

In this cry for freedom which reverberates around the world is the recognition of oppressed peoples that theology, as it was handed to them by their colonial overlords, was unable to address with specificity and clarity the problem of identity that plagued them. Oppressed peoples began to discover that their search in history for God was at the same time the search for self, and their search for self was often the search for God. So God became for them the one whom they encountered in history as freedom. God became the freeing one who, even in the midst of human bondage, signaled to them that they were meant for freedom.

This book is an attempt to relate Caribbean spirituality to other Third World experiences. The point of departure for reflection on the Caribbean experience will be my own background within the church in Jamaica. My knowledge of theological education and life as a pastor in the church in Jamaica indicated that theology as it was practiced within the church did not address the identity problem that slavery created among Caribbean peoples. God as presented within the Caribbean church was often not the symbol of freedom but, rather, the extension of the European and the North American church experience. I recall praying within the church in Jamaica, "Lord, wash me until I am whiter than snow." In the Caribbean, hymns as well as liturgies and theology have been mainly imported from Europe and North America. The central problem here is not that imports may not have a place in Caribbean spirituality but that God, when understood through the medium of other peoples' experience, is in danger of losing identity for oppressed peoples. To interpret God in that way is to risk making God a foreigner to the consciousness of oppressed people.

1

It was therefore in the light of this background that I undertook to investigate from a Caribbean perspective oppressed peoples and their God in history and to discover what light, if any, other Third World experiences shed on the search for identity.

APPROACHES TO THE SUBJECT

There are three levels at which to consider approaches to the subject. First, I shall examine black America's articulation of black theology to discover if there are any lessons one can learn in the Caribbean from the relation between identity and religion. I study the relevance of black theology to the Caribbean situation for a number of reasons. First, the geographical proximity of the Caribbean and the United States is significant in terms of social development. Second, during slavery black people were often taken from the Caribbean islands to the United States; as they came they brought important elements for black American culture. Finally, and perhaps most importantly, black people in the Caribbean and the United States share a common experience, which may be characterized as the search for freedom in history.

The second approach asks what clues, if any, the Third World* offers those in the Caribbean who seek to reflect upon their religious experience. I have sought to differentiate between black America and the Third World because black people in America come out of a history that has been marked by the American experience. In the words of Arnold Rose:

The "Negro race" is defined in America by white people. Everybody having a *known* trace of Negro blood—no matter how far back it was acquired—is classified as a Negro. No amount of white ancestry, except one hundred percent, will permit entrance to the white race. This definition of the Negro race in the United States is different from that held in the rest of the American Continent. "In Latin America whoever is not black is white: in teutonic America whoever is not white is black." In the British colonies and dominions, primarily South Africa, the hybrids (half-castes) are considered as a group distinct from both white and Negroes. . . . This social definition of the Negro race, even if it does not change anything in the biological situation, increases the number of individuals included in the Negro race. It relegates a larger number of individuals who look like white

---

* The term "Third World" refers in this context to countries outside the industrialized, capitalist countries of Europe and North America, as well as Japan, Australia, and New Zealand, and the Socialist countries of Europe including the USSR. For a more complete definition of this concept, see the Final Statement of the Ecumenical Dialogue of Third World Theologians, Dar es Salaam, August 12, 1976, in Sergio Torres and Virginia Fabella, M.M., eds., *The Emergent Gospel* (Maryknoll, N.Y.: Orbis Books, 1978), pp. 259ff.

people, or almost so, to the Negro race. . . . But a few American Negroes also have the clearest of white skin, the bluest of blue eyes, and many have the long and narrow head that happens to be both a Negro and a "Nordic" trait.[1]

This distinctiveness of the black American experience warrants looking at the Third World perspective in its own right.

The third approach will look at works related to the Caribbean perspective. This dimension will indicate trends in the Caribbean to which the investigation will be related.

BLACK THEOLOGY

In *Black Awareness*, Major Jones points out that there are several interpretations black Americans have of black theology. It is an indispensable part of the "black revolution" in which black America is involved. In a context in which theology is the domain of white people, black theology is protest against the traditional way in which theology is done. According to Jones, "Black Theology differs from traditional theology by the simple reason that it may not be concerned to describe traditional themes as the external nature of God's existence as it is to explore the impermanent, paradoxical, and problematic nature of human existence."[2] Hence, an important task of black theology is the reclaiming of black America from humiliation.

The black experience is an important source for Jones in his articulation of black theology. Any theology in North America that ignores this experience runs the risk of being irrelevant. This relevance is emphasized in the statement made by the National Committee of Black Churchmen at the Interdenominational Theological Center in Atlanta, Georgia, June 13, 1969:

Black Theology is a theology of black liberation. It seeks to plumb the black condition in the light of God's revelation in Jesus Christ, so that the black community can see that the gospel is commensurate with the achievement of black humanity. Black Theology is a theology of "blackness."[3]

Insofar as the black experience is taken seriously as a datum of theological reflection, black theology becomes a theology of hope for oppressed people.

In his more recent book, *Christian Ethics for Black Theology*, Jones maintains that the uniqueness of the black experience forces the black Christian to give an answer different from that of the white Christian confronted with the question: "What ought I to do?" According to Jones: "The answer to this question depends on who is asking the question, and the answer may be made in the light of what the person has become. If he is black, the answer might be one thing; if he is white, it might be quite another."[4] So Jones concludes that black theology is not only a protest against the neglect of the black American experience by white theologians, but, because it takes this experience seriously, it constitutes a new point of departure for theology.

J. Deotis Roberts, Sr., speaks to some of Jones's concerns in pointing out how the identity of the black community is given. He sharpens the focus:

> The black man in recent years has become color-conscious in the sense that he is aware that he is black and that to the white majority, which controls both the wealth and power in this country, he is not equal. This means that any white man, however poor or illiterate, may assume superiority over any black man whatever his wealth, education, or position. Prejudice is a prejudgment at sight, and the black man is highly visible.[5]

According to Roberts, the central theological problem confronting American Christianity is racism. This phenomenon forces black Christians to ask for the relationship between black consciousness and theology. "The black man, who lives in the dark ghetto, in a rented shack and who works under a white boss, whose environment is regulated from city hall, whose landlord is white or Jewish and lives in the suburbs, lives an other-directed, powerless life. What does the Christian understanding of God say to this man whose life is controlled by a white landlord, a white boss, and white politicians?"[6] The immediate task of black people in America, explains Roberts, is black solidarity and black dignity. "When we know our identity, have gained our self-respect, and are fully confident as a people, we will be in a position to be reconciled to others as equals and not as subordinates. If we can take our black consciousness up into our Christian faith, we will find it not only unmanly but unchristian to be reconciled on less than an equal basis."[7]

Both Jones and Roberts have called attention to the many points at which Christianity and the black experience meet. Roberts contends that black people who have rejected Christianity are not consistent with the spiritual heritage they received as children. However, neither of them has pointed out that the Christianity which emerged and developed in the black church is of a different dimension from that which evolved in the white church. Neither Jones nor Roberts sought to uncover the "roots" of black religion, which would illuminate the search for black identity in America.[8] This distinction points to the cardinal difference between this present investigation of religion and identity in the Caribbean and the articulation of black theology in North America.[9] The memory in black history and black culture is significant for this investigation of religion and identity in the Caribbean.

John Mbiti of Africa cautions against an uncritical acceptance of black theology:

In Southern Africa Black Theology deserves a hearing, though it is impossible to see how that hearing could be translated into practical action. But even in Southern Africa the people need and want liberation, not a theology of liberation. America can afford to talk loud about liberation, for people are free enough to do that in America. But in Southern Africa people are not free enough to talk about the theology of liberation. . . .

Apart from Southern Africa the concerns of Black Theology differ considerably from those of African theology. . . . Black Theology hardly knows the situation of Christians living in Africa, and therefore its direct relevance for Africa is either nonexistent or only accidental.[10]

However, I am more hopeful than John Mbiti and suggest that black theology may be able to provide clues in the Caribbean as we seek to understand the quest of oppressed people for freedom in history. I say this because of the *common* quest in the Caribbean and in North America for liberation.

A THIRD WORLD PERSPECTIVE

The Caribbean falls within the ambit of Third World countries and as such shares a common history with these countries—a common history in which the European search for the expansion of empire and religious freedom brought Third World countries under political, economic, cultural, and religious domination by European people. The European zeal to "Christianize" and "civilize" the world often provided a rationale for Third World oppression. A statement issued by Third World theologians who met at Dar es Salaam, Tanzania, in August 1976, reported:

[Europeans] plundered the riches of the Americas, Asia, and Africa. Gold, silver, precious stones, and raw materials were taken to add enormously to their capital accumulation. Their countries grew in wealth and power by the underdevelopment of these conquered and colonized countries.[11]

In the Caribbean, Latin America, and Africa, the Europeans subjected the local population to their domination. "Only a few countries like Thailand and the hinterland of China escaped this process. The Russians on the other hand expanded Southward and Eastward up to Alaska." These dominated countries were required to produce sugar, labor, raw materials, and markets for the mother countries. "They forcibly expropriated fertile lands of the oppressed peoples, set up plantations of sugar, coffee, tea, rubber, etc. . . . They transported millions of peoples from one country to another to serve as slaves or indentured labour. Thus we have the Black population in the Americas and the Indians in Africa, Malaysia, Sri Lanka, and the

Pacific and Caribbean Islands.''[12] For centuries the people of Western Europe oppressed the people of the Caribbean, Latin America, Asia, and Africa.

It was unfortunate that the Christian churches were an important part of this process of domination. Very often their insistence that Christianity was a superior religion provided a rationale for the conquest and domination of so-called pagan peoples. In more overt ways the Christian church often used theology to undergird the system of oppression.

In an attempt to break the chains of oppression numerous Third World countries have begun to experiment with modified versions of socialism. Cuba, Jamaica, North Vietnam, and North Korea are examples. In Africa, Mozambique, Guinea-Bissau, and Angola are seeking a self-reliant socialist development. Tanzania is attempting a socialist/free enterprise approach.

Many countries of the Third World have begun to develop indigenous theologies in an attempt to counter oppression and give religious expression to an experience that takes their history seriously. In Africa, Latin America, Asia, and the Caribbean these theologies emerge from particular historical experiences. Commenting on the Latin American scene, Paulo Freire says:

> Many Latin American theologians who are today becoming more and more historically involved with the oppressed, rightly speak of a political theology of liberation rather than one of modernizing "development." These theologians can really begin to speak to the troubling questions of a generation which chooses revolutionary change rather than reconciliation of irreconcilables.[13]

The oppressed must refuse to be mere spectators in history, according to Freire. They must make history. "So the dramatic tension between the past and the future, death and life, being and non-being, is no longer a kind of dead end for me. I can see it for what it really is: a permanent challenge to which I must respond. And my response can be none other than my historical praxis—in other words, revolutionary praxis. . . . History is . . . a human event."[14]

Perhaps the most articulate voice among the theologians in Latin America is that of the Peruvian Gustavo Gutiérrez. He states that liberation theology in Latin America "is a theological reflection born of the experience of shared efforts to abolish the current unjust situation and to build a society, freer and more human."[15] The Latin American scene points to a meaningful shift in the church's commitment to oppressed peoples. "As theology seeks to reflect on the presence and action of the Christian in the world it must go beyond the visible boundaries of the Church. There must be an openness to the world. Instead of using only revelation and tradition as starting points as classical theology has done, it must start with facts and questions derived from the world and from history."[16] Indeed, this reflects a radical shift of emphasis when one recalls that in the process of colonization many churches were often partners with the oppressors in consigning the poor and powerless people to a status of "peoplelessness." Evidence of this change is seen as many churches are today involved in the struggle for economic justice and human dignity against political and economic oppression.

In Asia and Africa there is an intense interest in discovering the ways in which the study of traditional religions and the formation of indigenous theologies will help to humanize history. Yoshinobu Kumazawa, in "Where Theology Seeks to Integrate Text and Context," expresses it this way:

> At least two basic concepts, or traditions, can be distinguished when we discuss indigenization as a theological problem. One is indigenization as "planting" such as the Roman Catholic *plantatio ecclesiae,* and the other is indigenization as "participating" in the *missio Dei.* Behind the first type of indigenization as planting we find the basic structure of God-Church-World. This means that God's act for the world is always mediated by the Church. . . . The second type of indigenization as participation tries to overcome these problems. It has the structure of God-World-Church. This approach recognizes that God works in non-Christian countries as he does in Christian ones. The problem is to find a way to participate in his work. Indigenization is the effort to find a way to participate in his work.[17]

Thus as Christians in Asia join Christ and participate in his mission, an integration of text and context occurs. Asian theology, then, is primarily concerned with liberation from the colonial oppression both in religious and in sociopolitical terms as it seeks to become indigenous. It is of interest that the title of the report of the Asian Christian Youth Consultation for Development in Hong Kong in 1970 is "Lead Us Not into Imitation." Here the emphasis is liberation from the Western lifestyle.

In an essay published by the Urban Rural Mission, Christian Conference of Asia, "Theology as Historical Thinking," the Christian Conference of Asia pleads that theology in Asia should not merely reflect the Western way of doing theology but that there should be a thoroughgoing grounding of Asian theology in history:

> The historical struggle of Asian peoples must be the locus of theological reflection. The central locus of the historical struggle of Asian peoples for the transformation of inhuman and enslaving structures of Asian societies is outside the Asian churches; the churches [in] Asia are often alienated from the central thrust of Asian peoples' unfolding history.[18]

The Christian Conference of Asia cautioned that unless theology in Asia becomes indigenous it will remain alien and irrelevant:

> Any theological thinking that is aloof from the aspirations of Asian peoples and the goals of Asian societies cannot help but be alienated from the historical struggle of Asian peoples. . . . Therefore, . . . theological categories that are formed outside of the experiences of historical struggle are severely limited, if not outright distorted, even when they are "indigenised" or "contextualized." The power of theological language comes . . . through the struggle of the people for historical transformation.[19]

What are some of the clues that Africa holds for those in the Caribbean? In 1966 a consultation of African theologians was held at Immanuel College, Ibadan, Nigeria, under the auspices of the All Africa Conference of Churches. The consultation was the expression of a great need and longing that the churches of Africa would have the opportunity to think together about the Christian faith, which they had received from the West mainly through missionaries of a different cultural background. The consultation noted that the missionaries were unable to understand the reactions of young converts who sought to interpret Christian faith in the light of African traditional beliefs and practices. The consultation represented an attempt to ground theology in African culture, calling attention to the fact that "over a long period of growth the church had taken root in Africa and there were indications that here and there individuals were beginning to examine the heritage of the Church to see how pertinently it related to African thought, ideas and life in a rapidly changing situation."[20]

The All Africa Conference of Churches maintained that the time had come for the church in Africa to engage in original meditation. Professor Bolaji Idowu writes:

> It has become increasingly clear, and disturbingly so, that the Church has been speaking in Africa and to Africans in strange or partially understood tongues. We must be thankful to God that in spite of man's weaknesses and shortsightedness, the miracle of Grace has been taking place all over Africa. Nevertheless, we realize that both the tools and the method of evangelism as employed in the continent are now calling very loudly for a careful overhauling.[21]

Idowu further indicated that the way of doing theology in the past in Africa was informed by the assumption that Africa had nothing to contribute on either a cultural or a spiritual basis. As a consequence, the crucial problem confronting the church in Africa today is the "foreignness of Christianity." This has meant that the church in Africa has taught and preached about a strange God whom Africans identify as the God of white people. The dissatisfaction with this foreign God has led Africans to inquire concerning the God of their fathers, the God whom their ancestors worshiped in African traditional religion. The All Africa Conference of Churches concluded: ". . . we have left them with two Gods in their hands and thus made of them peoples of ambivalent spiritual lives."[22]

What, then, is African theology? John Mbiti speaks of it as "an understanding of the Faith according to the total situation of our peoples— historical, cultural, contemporary and anticipated or possible future."[23] Idowu refers to African theology as "Faith-in-self-expression."[24]

Fashole-Luke's "African Christian Theology" builds on the themes suggested by Mbiti and Idowu by pointing out that African Christian theology is

> an attempt to underline the point that conversion to Christianity must be coupled with cultural continuity. If Christianity is to be universally accepted in Africa, then it must become incarnate in the life and thought of Africa. It involves steeping oneself in the patterns of thought of traditional African religions and studying Christianity in the light of that heritage, thus endeavoring to find points of contact between African traditional beliefs and Christian beliefs, so that Christianity can be more effectively and relevantly proclaimed to the African situation.[25]

This, in broad outline, is something of the general context in which Third World countries and black America are involved in the search for freedom in history. It is not intended to be comprehensive, but to call attention to the larger context in which this investigation of religion and identity in the Caribbean will be in dialogue from time to time. However, before seeking possible clues relating to the study of the oppressed and their God in history, we must examine the approaches that have been made toward the subject from a Caribbean perspective.

After a brief visit to Jamaica in 1942, J. Merle Davis wrote a book entitled *The Church in the New Jamaica*. It is significant for this study for two reasons. First, Davis called on the church in Jamaica to be more cognizant of the fact that, with the exception of Haiti, Jamaica had the largest proportion of pure African stock of any country in the Western hemisphere, and the smallest percentage of white people. Davis comments:

> Under Spanish occupation, the native Arawak Indians had disappeared, and the estates were worked by great numbers of Negro slaves brought from the West Coast of Africa. . . . When the slave trade was abolished in 1807 there were 319,351 slaves in Jamaica. As a result of this extensive importation of Negroes, Jamaica has one of the highest ratios of Africans in its population of all the countries of the Western Hemisphere. This is variously estimated from 90 to 95 percent, and, if the coloured people were included, would amount to 98 percent of the population of the Island.[26]

The Church in the New Jamaica mistakenly identified the central problem of Jamaican spirituality as concubinage: "It challenges both the state and the community. The vast number of fatherless, virtually helpless, families which result from the man's repudiation of responsibility for the support of his children creates widespread economic distress and pushes a very large part of the population deep into poverty and pauperism."[27] Had Davis researched the African roots of black Jamaica to which he alluded, he would have noted that slavery created the problem of identity in Jamaica and that concubinage was one method by which the black family survived the world of slavery. Davis's treatment of black Jamaica was much too cursory to suggest answers to the problem of identity, yet it remains important because it raises significant issues for the Caribbean.

The Jamaica Council of Churches in 1951 published a book entitled *Christ for Jamaica*. Whereas *The Church in the New Jamaica* was primarily an attempt to isolate the social and economic ills affecting Jamaica, *Christ for Jamaica* sought to present Jesus Christ as the answer to the problem confronting Jamaica.

> As we write these words all the energies of the Council are bent towards bringing the message of the Gospel to all people in our land. In an Island, nominally Christian, great numbers of our people do not heed the claim of the Lord Jesus Christ and of his Church upon their lives. The hunger for a "new Jamaica" and a better way of life is there—but how shall it be satisfied? One thing we know—the answer is summed up in the words "Christ for Jamaica."[28]

The basic problem with this approach is that *Christ for Jamaica* sought to give the answer without dealing in any substantive way with the question. If Jesus is the answer, what is the question? Because of its failure to deal with the issues confronting Jamaican and Caribbean society, the book represents a simplistic attempt to present the answer without investigating what difference, if any, Jesus Christ makes in the Jamaican and Caribbean quest for identity. For the present study, the significance of the book is its relationship to this investigation of the oppressed in their search for freedom in history to discover whether or not Jesus is the answer to the problem of identity in the Caribbean.

An important contribution to the study of religion and identity in the Caribbean is Leonard Barrett's *Soul-Force*. The work is mainly an expansion of Barrett's earlier book, *Rastafarianism*, published in 1968. *Soul-Force* is significant for the Caribbean primarily because of the author's intimate knowledge of the Caribbean cults of Revivalism and Rastafarianism. Barrett insists that the study of religion in the Caribbean must take these cults seriously.

> It would be a formidable task for one to provide a detailed study of the various African traditional religions which have come down to the

present day. But it cannot be denied that these religious systems, which are usually called cults in our day, were so well established that, despite the onslaught of the European ruling class with their numerous laws aimed at eradicating them, and despite the onslaught of the European missionaries who spent their lives and their financial resources in an attempt to convert the slaves to Christianity, these New World African religions have remained to this day as the psychic monitors of the vast majority of New World Blacks.[29]

Barrett concludes that the answer to the problem of identity in the Caribbean will not come from within the church, but from outside. For him, the answer lies in the study of the Messianic cults. In this investigation I shall take Barrett's claim seriously and inquire concerning the future of the Caribbean church as a possible context in which the oppressed can find meaning.

In 1973 the Caribbean Conference of Churches published a collection of essays entitled *Troubling of the Waters*, edited by Idris Hamid. This is perhaps the most significant theological work to have appeared in the Caribbean in the last decade. *Troubling of the Waters*, which has contributors from most of the English-speaking Caribbean, states the problem of humanity in the Caribbean as the problem of identity. Idris Hamid illustrates the problem:

> God is really foreign to us. In the religious imagination of our people he is a . . . foreigner. . . . Even the categories of our religious experiences are imports which do not reflect our cultural and native experiences. We experience God as an outsider.[30]

The Reverend Ashley Smith, in "The Religious Significance of Black Power in Caribbean Churches," puts the problem in perspective:

> Walter Rodney's statement, "The adult black in our West Indian society is fully conditioned to thinking white". . . applies no less to the sphere of religion than it does in other aspects of Caribbean life. The intensity of black self-hatred, body-shame and fatalism is due mainly to the use of religion as an instrument for the inculcation of the "white bias" in the non-European peoples of the region. There must be few geo-political situations in which the Christian Church has so conformed to the principle of the socio-cultural compatibility as in the case of the Caribbean.[31]

Troubling of the Waters outlines many ways in which the Caribbean church has contributed to the problem of identity and suggests that as the church identifies unequivocally with the oppressed it will become the context within which the identity problem can be resolved. The book's main task is to indicate the common search for identity among Caribbean people.

Hence, *Troubling of the Waters* is extremely helpful in the breadth of its concerns for Caribbean humanity, but it does not deal in any significant way with the history and theology of Caribbean spirituality.

Troubling of the Waters is not a search for roots, but an attempt to indicate areas in which further research is needed in Caribbean history and spirituality. This present investigation is in part a response to *Troubling of the Waters* as the study of oppressed people and their search for freedom in history seeks to provide a window through which many Caribbean peoples will be able to see themselves and hence better understand their quest to be more fully human.

The focus of this book has been narrowed to the smaller circle to which this inquiry relates, that is, the Caribbean. But we must now ask about the possible relationship of this investigation to the larger circle, black America and the Third World countries. Ashley Smith's discussion of "The Religious Significance of Black Power in Caribbean Churches" suggests that there are few situations in which the church's captivity to culture is as pronounced as the Caribbean. However, listening to voices from the larger circle—Asia, Africa, Latin America, and black America—it becomes clear that there are points at which these two circles meet.

Professor John McNab, one time tutor at the United Theological Colleges of the West Indies, offers a word of caution:

> Black theology is as sectarian as Anglican, Roman Catholic and Reformed theologies which have been implanted on us by our Colonial missionaries. U.T.C.W.I. has served to expose that bondage to me, and I have no desire to be enslaved by another imported servitude. . . . I strongly suspect that Black Theology is another uncritical importation which affirms the self-deception that West Indians cannot think for themselves but must continue to imitate our North American benefactors.[32]

Caribbeans must take McNab's concern seriously and not imitate their black sisters and brothers in North America. However, it seems clear that some of those concerns are mutual. The quest for black identity is not peculiar to black America; neither is the recognition that the church often sided with the powers that be to keep black people in bondage. The cry for black liberation that exudes from James Cone's *A Black Theology of Liberation*[33] is also the cry that goes forth from oppressed peoples in the Caribbean. Perhaps it is appropriate in the light of this common cry for freedom to ask if black theology's relating of the biblical category of liberation to the sociopolitical cry for liberation offers any possible clues to this investigation.

Professor McNab's comment is also instructive for the inquiry as it considers the relationship of this investigation to other theologies. The theologies and liturgies belonging to the life and faith of the Caribbean church were, as noted earlier, mainly extensions of the European and North American churches' experience. Also, in Africa, Asia, and Latin America oppressed peoples were sometimes forced to ignore their indigenous religious traditions and beliefs as they were introduced to the Christian God.

Religious and theological trends in black America and Third World countries exhibit an unwillingness of oppressed peoples to live without their history and an insistence that their reflections about their God and themselves be within the context of "historical thinking." Oppressed peoples of the Caribbean, Africa, Latin America, Asia, and North America have begun to insist that their past must no longer leap over the present into the future but, rather, their future hopes must ever fashion the present out of the past.

These are some of the points at which these two circles intersect, and, as the study unfolds, the many areas in which the oppressed participate in a common heritage will become increasingly clear.

NOTES

1. Arnold Rose, *The Negro in America* (New York: Harper & Row Torchbooks, 1964), p. 42.

2. Major Jones, *Black Awareness* (Nashville: Abingdon, 1971), pp. 11–17, quotation from p. 14. Cecil Cone's *The Identity Crisis in Black Theology* (Nashville: AMEC, 1975) goes further than Jones's approach and suggests black religion as the foundation of black theology.

3. For complete text, see Gayraud S. Wilmore and James H. Cone, eds., *Black Theology: A Documentary History, 1966–1979* (Maryknoll, N.Y.: Orbis Books, 1979), pp. 100–102.

4. Major Jones, *Christian Ethics for Black Theology* (Nashville: Abingdon, 1974), p. 16.

5. Deotis Roberts, "Black Consciousness in Theological Perspective," in J. Gardiner and Deotis Roberts, Sr., eds., *Quest for a Black Theology* (Philadelphia: United Church Press, 1971), p. 64.

6. Ibid., p. 72.

7. Ibid., p. 79. For a more adequate treatment of black consciousness and reconciliation in Roberts's thought, see his *Liberation and Reconciliation* (Philadelphia: Westminster Press, 1974).

8. Both Joseph Washington in *Black Religion* (Boston: Beacon Press, 1972) and Gayraud S. Wilmore in *Black Religion and Black Radicalism* (New York: Doubleday, 1972) attempt this.

9. This observation would also be true of the early writings of James H. Cone, one of black America's foremost theologians. This is especially evident in *Black Theology and Black Power* (New York: Seabury, 1969), and *A Black Theology of Liberation* (Philadelphia: J. B. Lippincott, 1970). His more recent work, *God of the Oppressed* (New York: Seabury, 1975), indicates a serious attempt to allow black history and culture to shape the theological task.

10. John Mbiti, "An African Views American Black Theology," *Worldview*, August 1974, p. 43. See James Cone's response in "A Black American Perspective on the Future of African Theology," *African Theological Journal* 7, no. 2 (1978). Both papers are available in Wilmore and Cone, eds., *Black Theology*.

11. See Sergio Torres and Virginia Fabella, eds., *The Emergent Gospel* (Maryknoll, N.Y.: Orbis Books, 1978), pp. 260–61.

12. Ibid., p. 4. Allan Boesak, *Farewell to Innocence* (Maryknoll, N.Y.: Orbis Books, 1977), and Basil Moore, ed., *The Challenge of Black Theology in South Africa* (Atlanta: John Knox, 1974), support this interpretation.

13. See Paulo Freire, "Education, Liberation and the Church," *Risk* 9, no. 2 (1973): 38. See also Paulo Freire's *Pedagogy of the Oppressed* (New York: Seabury, 1973), which is an important contribution to Latin American liberation. José Míguez Bonino, *Doing Theology in a Revolutionary Situation* (Philadelphia: Fortress Press, 1975), and Enrique Dussel, *History and the Theology of Liberation* (Maryknoll, N.Y.: Orbis Books, 1976), support Freire's claim.

14. See Freire, "Education," p. 39.

15. See Gustavo Gutiérrez, *A Theology of Liberation* (Maryknoll, N.Y.: Orbis Books, 1973), p. ix.

16. Ibid., p. 12. For a helpful interpretation of liberation theology, see Robert McAfee Brown, *Theology in a New Key* (Philadelphia: Westminster Press, 1978).

17. Yoshinobu Kumazawa, "Where Theology Seeks to Integrate Text and Context," in Gerald H. Anderson, ed., *Asian Voices in Christian Theology* (Maryknoll, N.Y.: Orbis Books, 1976), p. 204. Gerald Anderson and Thomas Stransky, eds., *Mission Trends*, nos. 1–4 (New York, Grand Rapids: Paulist Press and Wm. B. Eerdmans Publishing Co., 1974–79), provide a helpful framework to futher interpret Kumazawa's approach to theology.

18. See "Theology as Historical Thinking," Appendix 2 in *Towards a Theology of People,* Oh Jae Shik, ed. (Tokyo: Urban Rural Mission, Christian Conference of Asia, 1977), p. 172.

19. Ibid., p. 175. See also Choan-Seng Song, *Christian Mission in Reconstruction* (Maryknoll, N.Y.: Orbis Books, 1977).

20. Kwesi Dickson and Paul Ellingworth, eds., *Biblical Revelation and African Beliefs* (Maryknoll, N.Y.: Orbis Books, 1973), p. vii.

21. "Introduction," in ibid., p. 9.

22. Ibid., p. 34.

23. See John Mbiti, "African Theology," *Worldview* 16, no. 8 (August 1973): 38.

24. See Bolaji Idowu, *African Traditional Religion* (Maryknoll, N.Y.: Orbis Books, 1973), p. 28.

25. See Edward W. Fashole-Luke, "African Christian Theology?" *Communio Viatorum* 17, no. 3 (Prague, Czechoslovakia, 1974).

26. See J. Merle Davis, *The Church in the New Jamaica* (New York–London: International Missionary Council, 1942), p. 3.

27. Ibid., p. 36.

28. See J. A. Crabb, ed., *Christ for Jamica* (Kingston, Jamaica: Pioneer Press, 1951), p. xii.

29. Leonard E. Barrett, *Soul-Force* (Garden City, N.Y.: Anchor Press/Doubleday, 1974), pp. 79–80.

30. See Idris Hamid, ed., *Troubling of the Waters* (San Fernando, Trinidad: Rahaman Printery, 1973), p. 8. Although I am aware of two recent publications by the Caribbean Conference of Churches—Idris Hamid, ed., *Out of the Depths* (San Fernando, Trinidad: Rahaman Printery, 1977), and Kortright Davis, ed., *Moving into Freedom* (Bridgetown, Barbados: Cedar Press, 1977)—they do not go beyond the scope of *Troubling of the Waters*.

31. Ashley Smith, in *Troubling of the Waters*, p. 44.

32. McNab, in ibid., p. 106.

33. James H. Cone, *A Black Theology of Liberation* (Philadelphia: J. B. Lippincott, 1970).

1

Black People and Their Search for Freedom

Like most people, the first Jamacians believed in a Supreme Being. "He was immortal, invisible, omnipotent but not uncreated, because he had a mother who presided either in the Sun or Moon. He was called by several names, chiefly by that of Jocahuna, and lived in the skies. . . ."[1]

The first Jamaicans (the Arawaks) were a religious people. Although Christopher Columbus was instructed by Queen Isabella and King Ferdinand of Spain to teach the first Jamaicans Christianity, his main purpose was not religious. Indeed, he had come to exploit, not to teach. This lust after riches led to the enslavement of the Arawak and engendered one of the most gruesome stories of the abuse of a people.

It is an error to say that Christopher Columbus discovered Jamaica. The Arawaks were there when he arrived. The cruelty the Spaniards meted out to them calls attention to the interruption of their history by Columbus. This interruption resulted in the decimation of the first Jamaicans by the Spaniards. According to historical estimates, the population of Jamaica was approximately 60,000 at the time Columbus arrived. A century later the number was 1,500, of whom 74 were Arawak.

In 1509 Juan de Esquivel, the first governor of Jamaica, was allowed to import three slaves, provided they were Christians. These were the first black people to be brought to Jamaica.[2] The two realities, blackness and Christianity, were to be noteworthy in the interpretation of the theological significance of humanity in Jamaica.

The importation of great numbers of black people as slaves in the Caribbean was a direct consequence of the church's intervention on behalf of oppressed people. In his celebrated work *The History, Civil and Commercial, of the British Colonies in the West Indies,* Bryan Edwards, the eighteenth-century historian, informs us that in 1517 Charles V of Spain granted permission for 4,000 black people to be brought annually to the islands of Hispaniola, Cuba, Jamaica, and Puerto Rico. The emperor

16

granted this request because of the pleading of the church. According to Edwards, "The concurrence of the emperor to this measure was obtained at the solicitation of Bartholomew de las Casas, Bishop of Chiapa, the celebrated protector of the Indians; and the conduct of this great prelate on that occasion has been the subject of much censure. . . . While he contended . . . for the liberty of the people born in one quarter of the globe, he laboured to enslave the inhabitants of another region and in the warmth and zeal to save the Americans from the yoke, pronounced it to be lawful and expedient to impose one, still heavier, upon the Africans."[3]

The basis of the church's action was called into question then, and today the church must continue to question the norms for its action. Is it the prior action of God in Jesus Christ, as the church claims? The action of the church seems to contradict its theological affirmation. For God in Christ cannot support slavery and oppression. Indeed, the primacy of the action of the God who is revealed in Jesus Christ would ensure the humaneness of the church's action. However, the church's action makes it responsible for the presence of black people in the Caribbean, their abuse, and their struggle to affirm their worth as children of freedom.

The unfolding of the history of the abuse of black people in the Caribbean brings to the fore a question the historian Bryan Edwards broaches when he asks, How may we talk about the love of God in the context of oppression? The action of the church and the question posed by Edwards place black people and the God of the Christian church irrevocably together in the Caribbean. How may we talk about God's love for these people? Edwards, in suggesting that the God whom the church proclaims will condemn all oppressive structures, wonders how this will be if the Christians' God is held captive by the church. Edwards could not resolve this contradiction.[4] However, we today should take Edwards seriously and ask about the Christians' God of love, the God of the church responsible for oppression. A clue to how one might talk about the love of God in the midst of oppression is found in Scripture's witness to the God who entered into a situation of oppression so that, through his suffering, the victims of oppression might experience his liberating love. The Christian interpretation of Isaiah 53 suggests a partial answer to Edward's question about the love of God in the midst of oppression.

He was oppressed, and he was afflicted,
yet he opened not his mouth;
like a lamb that is led to the slaughter,
and like a sheep that before its shearers is dumb,
so he opened not his mouth.
By oppression and judgment he was taken away;
and as for his generation,
who considered that he was cut off
out of the land of the living,

stricken for the transgression of my people?
And they made his grave with the wicked
and with a rich man in his death,
although he had done no violence,
and there was no deceit in his mouth. [Isa. 53:7–9, RSV]

In reading from Isaiah 61:1–2, Jesus interpreted his mission as being for the victims of oppression (Lk. 4:18–19). Martin Luther, a contemporary of Bartholomew de las Casas, stated in his *Heidelberg Disputation* that to know the love of God as it is revealed in Jesus Christ is to experience a God who is hidden in suffering: "God can only be found in suffering and the cross. . . ."[5] Therefore, Christian love proclaims that "God suffered in the suffering of Jesus, God died on the cross of Christ . . . so that we may live in the future."[6] Both Luther and Moltmann seem to suggest that God's love as it is revealed in Jesus Christ does not confirm and affirm the structures of death and bondage; on the contrary, his love shows the way out.

Edwards did not understand that Christian love proclaims not only a God who is for the church, but also a God who is against the church, as he stands over against the church in judgment. This seems to be the theological significance of Matthew 25:35–46. Whenever the church participates in denying people the right to be human, it is condemned by its God (Matt. 25:45–46).

In the meantime we are told by a Spanish priest that the population of black people increased in Jamaica. Giving a report based on the number of confessions he ordered in 1611, the priest reports: "In the whole island, from the note of the number of confessions that I ordered to be made this year, with particular care, there were 1,510 persons of all classes and conditions, 523 Spaniards including men and women, 173 children, 107 free negroes, 74 indians (Arawaks), natives of the Island, 558 slaves, and 75 foreigners."[7]

Spanish rule came to an end in 1655 when the British captured Jamaica. With the arrival of the British, the Spaniards freed their slaves and fled to Cuba. When the British captured Jamaica there were about 1,500 Africans who in claiming their freedom took to the hills, from where they would descend to attack the British.[8]

It is of interest that black people during this period were compared with the children of Israel in Egypt, foreigners in a strange land, abused by Europeans.[9] Black people in Jamaica were confronted with a people, a God, and a culture that were strange to them. Black people had to learn a new language and discover the strange ways of the God of their masters.

Dehumanization of black people took many forms in the system of slavery. One account tells of a black family called to work each morning by the blowing of a shell. The overseer, carrying a long whip, led them to the fields. Children as young as six years old worked in the pastures. The family had to work from "sun up until sun down." Sometimes they had to return at night to work by the light of the moon. If, upon examination, the overseer was dissatisfied with any part of the work, the laborer responsible —whether man or woman—was flogged until blood ran. The cracking of the whip and the shrieks of the victims were heard nightly.[10]

One of the most degrading indignities of this period was that the entire black family was enslaved. Even little children were victims. The deprivations which the black family had to endure were not only those inflicted on their bodies, but those inflicted on their personalities. The sense of community—so important to the African family—was destroyed. In the world made for black people by the slaveholder, the children of the black family became the property of the master. Every attempt was made to denude the black families of their identity and any sense of responsibility within their community. Often slaves of the same family or tribe were separated from each other and had their names changed several times, the more surely to destroy their identity and their humanity.

It must not be thought that the abuse of black people was unique to Jamaica. The trade in black people, which developed in the seventeenth and eighteenth centuries, was mainly in the hands of the Dutch, French, and English. The Dutch West India Company, which was organized in 1621, established trade between Africa and the Dutch colonies in the New World. Holland had the advantage over England in slave trade in the seventeenth century because England was often distracted with civil wars at home. During this time Dutch ships could be seen in almost every port in the New World. They sold black people as slaves in Martinique, Guadeloupe, and, on occasion, even in the Spanish islands.[11] Both in South America and in the West Indies, Holland used its colonies as centers for the distribution of slaves throughout the New World.

In a world in which black humanity was defined as property, one can begin to understand something of the poor image of the self that emerges among black people. The prime minister of Jamaica, Michael Manley, in an address to the World Council of Churches in 1975, put the problem into perspective:

> Let me remind you that liberation is about victims. . . . Every family that is undernourished is a victim. Not only the unemployed, but every man and woman whose work is underpaid, irregular or insecure are victims. And every child born of unions of such men and women are doubly victimized; for they do not only have to suffer malnutrition, disease, overcrowded living conditions or actual homelessness, desertion by parents or orphanhood, ignorance and talents stunted by starvation . . . they also suffer the crippling effects of insecurity and the deprivation of love. . . . Every person who has been denied equality, who has been treated with less than full regard, who has been maimed or killed, because of race or religion, is a victim.[12]

The history of the abuse of black people recounted here suggests that the fear of losing the freedom to be fully human is a mirror through which many oppressed peoples can see their histories reflected. Gayraud S. Wilmore notes the problem of identity that slavery created:

> Even under the most favorable conditions, Black slavery in the New World was a deliberate system of cultural and psychological genocide. Every connection with the past was to be obliterated and the slaves were to be so thoroughly dehumanized and brainwashed that they would forget that he or she had been anything other than Nigger John or Nigger Mandy created by God, as the early slave catechism's taught, to "make a crop."[13]

The religious argument that God made black people slaves in order to "make a crop" was one method of justifying a system that sought to rob them of their identity and of the freedom to become more fully human.

However, in the midst of the abuse of their dignity and the denial of their rights to be a people before God, through memory the oppressed blacks rejected slave society and affirmed the community from which they came. For these people, to die was often to live. They were not afraid to die, because death meant the way home to their ancestors' land. So to die was to be reunited with their true community.[14] Memory was the basis of their hope.[15]

BLACK SLAVE AND WHITE SERVANT

The experience of human bondage was not unique to black people. White people in the seventeenth century in the Caribbean were also dehumanized by Europeans in the quest for economic power. In *The History of Jamaica* we read that

> great numbers used formerly to be brought from Scotland, where they were actually kidnapped by some *mantraders*, in or near Glasgow, and shipped for this island, to be sold for four or five years term of service. On their arrival, they used to be ranged in a line, like new Negroes, for the planters to pick and choose. . . . Many of these menial servants, who are retained for the sake of saving a deficiency, are the very dregs of the three kingdoms. They have commonly more vices, and much fewer good qualities, than the slaves over whom they are set in authority; the better sort of which heartily despise them, perceiving little or no difference from themselves, except in skin, and blacker depravity.[16]

As one ponders the religious argument that God made black people "to make a crop," which was used to set up a distance between black slave and white servant in the Caribbean, it seems clear that racism was the very basis of the abuse of black people. A classic illustration of using theology as the basis for maintaining the servitude of black people is found in the words of Count Zinzendorf, the Moravian spiritual leader: "God punished the first Negroes by making them slaves, and your conversion will make you free, not from control of your masters, but simply from your wicked habits and thoughts, and all that makes you dissatisfied with your lot."[17]

There is an interesting difference between the black American's experience of slavery and that of the black Jamaicans. Apart from the fact that black oppression in Jamaica antedates the black American experience by over one hundred years,[18] it must be kept in mind that the first twenty black people who were left at Jamestown, Virginia, in 1619 were servants. From 1619 to 1665 black people and white people worked side by side in Virginia as servants. So there were black servants and white servants in North America.[19] However, according to John Hope Franklin, most black people who were taken to Virginia after 1640 were not given contracts as bonded servants and therefore had difficulty purchasing their freedom. "Some others who were brought in enjoyed the dubious distinction of having contracts, provided they were servants for life."[20] Winthrop Jordan supports Franklin's thesis that during the first half of the seventeenth century black people in America were servants and not slaves. He points out that although black people went to New York in 1628, it is quite likely that they remained free until after 1650.[21] Both Jordan and Franklin suggest that, in the second half of the seventeenth century, white indentured servanthood was phased out and both religious and racial arguments were developed to undergird black slavery in North America.

However, it must not be assumed that white people in North America did not regard black people as racially inferior until after 1650. As early as 1630 Hugh Davis was ordered to be soundly whipped "before an assembly of Negroes and others, for abusing himself to the dishonor of God and shame of Christians by defiling his body in lying with a negroe; which fault he is to acknowledge next Sabbath."[22]

Therefore, although the European in Jamaica dehumanized both black and white people, there were profound differences in the black slaves' and the white servants' experience of dehumanization. Black people were cheaper to buy than white people, and at worst the white person was an indentured servant for seven years. Black people were slaves for life. The master owned both the black slave and his children, whereas the children of white servants were always born free. To be born white was to be free. To be born black was to be a slave for life. Because of the racial difference, oppression of whites was soon phased out, but the master continued to abuse the black family. In the words of Eric Williams, "the great inhumanity of man to man" had its genesis in the zeal of white people to maintain the structure of master and slave.[23]

THE ESSENCE OF HUMANITY

What is it that makes a man a man? We reply, a consciousness of his responsibility to God and man, producing in him a feeling of self respect. But what responsibility to his creator . . . to his God, can a slave feel, when he in innumerable instances is forced to do what his conscience tells him is sin? What self respect can a slave have, when he finds himself the tool of another man's will? He knows nothing of those feelings which alone can make a man to be a man.[24]

These words from the Reverend J. H. Buchner focus, correctly, on the social context in which consciousness is shaped. And certainly one must take cognizance of the impact of the environment in the shaping of the self-image. This points to one of the problems confronting black people today. Long after the abolition of slavery they carry its memory and scars. Their estimate of themselves is still greatly influenced by the memory of slavery. Although black people may have rejected the history and the world that sought to reduce them to "peoplelessness," they are still not free of its formative influences.

After a visit to Jamaica, a contemporary writer pointed out that in 1973 the average per capita income was $719. Between 35 and 40 percent of the adult population is illiterate. The national unemployment rate is estimated to be higher than 30 percent, and this occasions the high crime rate. The writer, Bill Neckirk, cites a young woman as reporting of black people in Jamaica: "They just don't have anything to do. They are depressed. There are no jobs. Kingston is overpopulated. We have family planning programs, but many of our people are not educated enough to take advantage of it. Many of the run down houses have ten and eleven people living in them."[25] The world of black people that Buchner discussed in 1854 is similar to that which Neckirk described in 1976. In both worlds there does not seem to be much room for hope.

When black people's historical situation is related to the biblical situation of Israel, is it possible to make any theological sense out of their servitude and the apparent hopelessness that characterizes it? This is the critical question. In the Old Testament, we are told that Israel could hope in the midst of despair because Yahweh entered into their historical situation of bondage and transformed it into freedom. Freedom for Israel occurred in the context of oppression. Is not this experience possible for black people? Indeed, this is what happened. To say of the black people, "They know nothing of those feelings which alone can make a human being to be a human" is to close the door of faith and hence make no room for freedom. How else may one explain the many revolts and revolutions of black people in Haiti and Jamaica against a system that sought to deprive them of their freedom to be a people, except to acknowledge that they were not depraved and that in spite of the oppressive social context in which they lived, their faith in freedom persisted? History indeed shows that there was scarcely a week when black people in Jamaica did not protest their bondage.

Scripture is clear that the God who created the world guarantees the liberation of oppressed people.[26] The biblical view of humanity affirms that God's freedom challenges all forms of unfreedom. His freedom breaks the power of bondage. The children of Israel, like the victims of oppression in the Caribbean, were not free to be persons before their God. In confronting Pharaoh, Moses presented God's demand of freedom for his people: "And you shall say to him 'The Lord, the God of the Hebrews, sent me to you, saying, Let my people go, that they may serve me in the wilderness' " (Exod. 7:16, RSV).

To return to Buchner's question, "What is it that makes a man a man?" seems in the light of biblical religion to elicit the response that the essence of humanity is freedom. When black people's struggle to be more fully human is seen in the light of biblical religion, one sees how they begin to learn that the God of Israel listens to the cry of people who are victims and wills that they be set free.

In a world of oppression, victims are threatened by bondage, which seeks to break the power of freedom. The good news that biblical religion announces is that God's freedom breaks the power of bondage and offers to oppressed humanity the possibility to participate in their freedom. The witness of Scripture indicates that freedom must challenge human bondage in all its forms. The search of the oppressed for their God points to the unfolding of a drama between freedom and bondage, a contest between God and Baal (see 1 Kings 18).

THE COLOR PROBLEM

It is important to clarify the relationship between black people and other people in the Caribbean. This is critical because of the color problem, which was occasioned when the African and the European met in the New World. The meeting of these two peoples was an encounter of two histories, two traditions, and two approaches to religion. In the meeting of Europe and Africa, blackness was interpreted in the light of bondage, and whiteness in the light of freedom. Commenting on the color problem in the Caribbean, Bryan Edwards reports:

The poorest white person seems to consider himself nearly on a level with the richest, and emboldened by the idea, approaches his employer with extended hand and a freedom which in the countries of Europe is seldom displayed by men in the lower orders of life towards their superiors. It is not difficult to trace the origin of this principle. It arises without doubt from the pre-eminence and distinction which are necessarily attached even to the complexion of a white man, in a country where the complexion generally speaking distinguishes freedom from slavery.[27]

To be white was to be free and to be black was to be sentenced to bondage. It follows then, that because whiteness was the symbol of freedom, it became the ideal for black people. White people in Jamaica today number about 15,000 in a population approaching 2 million. The "white bias" in the Jamaican community came to the fore in black-white unions. The following gradations illustrate the problem:

Sambo: the child of a mulatto and a black man
Mulatto: the child of a black woman and a white man
Quadroon: the child of a mulatto and a white man
Mustee: the child of a quadroon and a white man
Mustiphini: the child of a mustee and a white man
Quintroon: the child of a mustiphini and a white man
Octoroon: the child of a quintroon and a white man [28]

The rationale behind this gradation was the obliteration of the "black stain." An octoroon was legally white, and therefore free, automatically in Jamaica.

The gradation calls attention to one of the essential differences between black people in the United States and black people in the Caribbean. In the Caribbean if a black man marries a white woman, his children will achieve a higher social status than those born from a black union.[29]

Is there any hope of black people reversing this pattern of interpreting themselves in the light of a white ideal? In recent years the Rastafarians, who acclaim the divinity of Haile Selassie, have been calling on black people to interpret their culture and history in the light of a black God.* The Rastafarians suggest that the blackness of God ensures the dignity and sanctity of black people.[30] Therefore blackness is no longer viewed as a stain or corruption; rather, it points to the humanity of God. The recounting of the history of black people and their God indicates that to be black is to be different. Perhaps on the basis of the blackness of God, black people will begin to accept their difference from other peoples.

NOTES

1. W. J. Gardner, *A History of Jamaica* (London: T. Fisher, 1873), p. 23.
2. Fernando Henriques, *Jamaica, Land of Wood and Water* (London: McGibbon S. Kee, 1957), p. 20.

*The Rastafarians, a Jamaican religious group who await the reincarnation of Haile Selassie I of Ethiopia, are discussed in chapter 6, below.

3. Bryan Edwards, *The History, Civil and Commercial, of the British Colonies in the West Indies* (London: Stockdale, 1801), vol. 1, pp. 38–39. It is of interest that Bartholomew de las Casas (1474–1566), who was in many ways the father of Caribbean theology, was a contemporary of Martin Luther and John Calvin.

4. Ibid., pp. 35–36.

5. Martin Luther, *Selected Writings of Martin Luther 1517–1520*, ed. Theodore G. Tapport (Philadelphia: Fortress Press, 1967), p. 79.

6. Jürgen Moltmann, *The Crucified God* (New York: Harper & Row, 1974), p. 216.

7. Henriques, *Jamaica*, p. 20.

8. Edwards, *History*, vol. 3, p. 303.

9. Cf. Edwards, *History*, vol. 2, p. 20. Gardner, *History*, p. 97.

10. See Leonard Tucker, *Glorious Liberty* (London: The Baptist Missionary Society, 1914), p. 6.

11. See John Hope Franklin, *From Slavery to Freedom* (New York: Vintage Books, 1969), p. 50.

12. Michael Manley, *From the Shackles of Domination and Oppression*, Address Document no. A8, World Council of Churches, Fifth Assembly, Nairobi, Kenya, 1975, p. 5. Manley has certainly crossed racial boundaries in his categorization of victims. I would agree with him that in Jamaica, as elsewhere, it is not only black people who are victims. However, I have chosen black people because, apart from being 90 percent of the population in Jamaica and being at the foot of the social and economic ladder, black people are most subject to the indignities and injustices to which Manley refers.

13. "Identity Crisis: Blacks in Predominantly White Denominations," in William Howard, ed., *Colloquium on Black Religion* (New York: Reformed Church in America, 1976), p. 5.

14. See Gardner, *History*, p. 99.

15. For an interpretation of the logic undergirding this position, see John Mbiti's *African Religions and Philosophy* (New York: Frederick A. Praeger, 1969), pp. 22–23.

16. Edward Long, *The History of Jamaica* (London: Lowndes, 1774), vol. 2, pp. 288–89.

17. Cited in Idris Hamid, ed., *Troubling of the Waters* (San Fernando, Trinidad: Rahaman Printery, 1973), p. 63. For a detailed account of the logic that informs this position, see also James McQueen, *The West Indies Colonies* (London: Hurst and Co., 1825).

18. See Henriques, *Jamaica*, p. 20. I pointed out above that black people were imported to Jamaica in 1509 provided they would become Christian slaves.

19. See Franklin, *From Slavery*, p. 48.

20. Ibid., p. 72.

21. Winthrop R. Jordan, *White over Black* (Baltimore: Penguin Books, 1973), p. 83.

22. H. Shelton Smith, *In His Image, But . . .* (Durham, N.C.: Duke University Press, 1972), p. 3.

23. Eric Williams, *The Negro in the Caribbean* (New York: Negro University Press, 1942), p. 11.

24. Rev. J. H. Buchner, *The Moravians in Jamaica* (London: Longman, Brown and Co., 1854), p. 20.

25. *Chicago Tribune*, January 10, 1976.

26. G. Ernest Wright, *The Old Testament and Theology* (New York: Harper & Row, 1969), p. 95.

27. Edwards, *History*, vol. 2, p. 7.

28. See Edward Brathwaite, *The Development of Creole Society in Jamaica 1770–1820* (Oxford: Clarendon Press, 1971), p. 167.

29. Fernando Henriques, *Family and Color in Jamaica* (London: Eyre and Spottiswood, 1953), p. 43; for an excellent treatment of the problem of color in Jamaica, see pp. 42–63.

30. Rex Nettleford, *Identity, Race and Protest in Jamaica* (New York: William Morrow, 1972), pp. 100–101.

2

Black People and Their World

A crucial aspect of black people's self-understanding is a great need to understand their world. In order for them to understand themselves better, they must look at the world from which they came and be willing to let their past world dialogue with their present world. Failure to look at their world combined with a lack of readiness to act upon it and transform it could lead to bondage in their world. Paul Tillich says that the self is transcendent when it does not merely respond to the impact of its environment, but actually shapes its world. "Without its world, the self would be an empty form."[1] One of the great challenges facing black people in Jamaica is to refuse to live in bondage to their world, as they are free to be creative interpreters of their world.

When one examines Jamaica in the eighteenth and early nineteenth centuries, one notes the distance between European culture as it was reflected in the plantocracy and black culture as it was practiced by Africans. It was a fact that the cultural heritage of black people in Jamaica was mainly African, which accounted for the presence of two worlds there. The African world was able to survive in Jamaica because Europeans "were more interested in indoctrinating the blacks with essential European techniques for saving souls and planting estates, than in understanding the culture of the Africans." Both the European and African worlds were alien to Jamaica. An important difference, however, was that whereas the European could maintain contact with Europe by returning to it and corresponding with people there, the African's only contact was with later shipments of slaves. However, as late as 1830 there were many black people in Jamaica who remembered Africa.[2]

THE WORLD FROM WHICH BLACK PEOPLE CAME

Because black people in Jamaica did not return to Africa and could not correspond with their families in black Africa, there were many adaptations of African beliefs to the Jamaican situation, as we shall see.

Black people in Jamaica came from different tribal and national groups in

27

Africa. The most numerous were the Karamante, or "Coromantyn" (the Ashanti-Fante people from the Gold Coast) and the Ibo from the Niger delta. There seems to have been a connection between the people and the region from which they came. The Karamante were considered stronger and hence better workers on the plantations, but were noted for initiating rebellions, and so were regarded as dangerous. The Ibo, on the other hand, were supposed to be given to suicide if ill treated. The great majority of black people in Jamaica had come from West Africa and represented only regional variations of a common world.

Since white people were not anxious to force Europeanization any further than was necessary for plantation work, black people were left to educate their children. The black woman became a vital link in communicating the black world to succeeding generations. By 1830 this process was solidly entrenched in Jamaica. Therefore the world from which black people came had decisively affected the world in which they searched for freedom in 1830.

The impact of the black world is seen in the attitude of black people in relation to Christian marriage. Black people were free to make whatever sexual relationships they needed, and these were usually permanent. The family unit was not dependent on the blessing of the established church. The wife had specific responsibilities within the family. She was in charge of marketing. She would serve her husband by cooking his meal, waiting on him, and then eating alone. While the black woman was willing to accept this lifestyle with its heavy responsibility, she was unwilling to accept Christian marriage.[3] The Christian concept of marriage was unknown to black people prior to the coming of the missionary, and black people refused to change their practice of concubinage for it. The black woman also tended to regard Christian marriage as a mark of subordination and slavery to the male. A large percentage of black Jamaica still rejects Christian marriage.

Another area in which one may clearly see the impact of the black world is in music and dance. Black people in Jamaica did not differentiate between the religious and the secular in music and dance. All of life had religious significance for black people. Hence there was a merging of the sacred and the secular in black religion.[4] Black people's ability to bring together the sacred and the secular in black religion is nowhere more clear than in their celebration of Christmas, which featured

the John Canoe dance. The chief performer wore traditional headdress in the form of a model boat looking something like a stylized Noah's ark. With . . . [a] wooden sword in his hand, he performed a dance through the streets of the town accompanied by a group of followers and musicians with *goombay* drums, gourds filled with the seeds of the Indian shot plant, and other African rhythmic instruments. Although the planters considered this harmless fun, and the missionaries objected mainly because of the rum-drinking involved, the John Canoe dance was in fact very closely associated with the survivals of African religion and magic. The figures represented in the houseboat—headdress, the phraseology of the songs, the instruments—all were very similar to those of the African cult groups that were otherwise driven underground.[5]

The Christmas celebration had special significance for black people, not because of Christian associations, but because they were allowed three days off from work by law and an opportunity to make a connection with the world from which they came.

Throughout the year the chief entertainments were of African derivation, which meant, of course, that the most important were dances. They were usually accompanied by a band, the instruments for which—the same as those for the John Canoe procession—were common in West Africa, and so was the pattern of leader and chorus singing.

It was in religion that Europeans worked hardest to influence black culture in the eighteenth and nineteenth centuries, and yet it is in religion that the survival of African culture is most noticeable in twentieth-century Jamaica. Two of the forms of black religion carried over from Africa to Jamaica were obeah and myalism.[6]

In Ashanti the word for witch or wizard is *obayifo,* and in Jamaica this became *obeah.* According to Howard Stroger, who has made a study of this, black Jamaica believed that the person who had the power of obeah had the ability to leave his body, to fly at night, and to cause great harm to befall the enemy. One of the main functions of the obeah-man was that of making poison with which he would kill the enemy.

The practice of obeah in Jamaica assumed a dimension of mystery. In part, this was because the slaves were forbidden by law to indulge in black religion and because the oppressive nature of plantation slavery did not lend itself to the accommodation of the slaves' practice of orthodox religion.[7] The obeah-man became invaluable to black people in Jamaica, as he offered them protection from the overseer or master, who had the right to whip, mutilate, or sell any slave at will. The obeah-man would give to the slave a charm to be worn to protect him against the cruelty of the master. Obeah served black people not only in protecting them from their masters, but as a means of taking revenge on a fellow slave. Because slaves were valuable property to the masters, they were forbidden to fight; the obeah-man served as the means of securing revenge when a black person was wronged by a member of his community. In a context in which slave women sometimes sought alliances with white men, the black man quite often had to depend on the obeah-man to " 'win the heart' of a woman for him."[8]

In a world fraught with fear and the pressure to conform, black people had to turn to the obeah-man for spiritual and practical help, and it is believed that every plantation had one or more obeah-men among its black personnel. Black people expressed the belief that the yoke of slavery was punishment by the gods of their religion. "In such a situation . . . the slave adopted a utilitarian approach to religion, accepting those portions of their traditional religion that were workable. . . ."[9]

M. G. Lewis, in his *Journal of a West Indian Proprietor*, in 1816 referred to Christianity as white obeah. The set of circumstances that led Lewis to make the connection between Christianity and black obeah had to do with the sense of powerlessness he as a white man experienced in the wake of black religion. He writes of an obeah-man called Adam who attempted to poison an attorney and discovered that his plan failed because Bessie, a black woman, betrayed him. So Adam cursed Bessie, and her health declined and her four children died, one after another. Lewis tried white obeah to counteract Adam on two levels. First, he suggested to Bessie "that her pickaninies were not dead forever, but were only gone up to live with God, who was good, and would take care of them for her; and that if she were good, when she dies, she too would go up to God above the blue, and see all her four pickaninnies again."[10] White obeah would work for Bessie if she were good, that is, if she served her master faithfully. The second thing that Lewis attempted in order to break the spell that Adam had over Bessie's family, and indeed over a great deal of his estate, was to Christianize Adam. Lewis writes:

> In short, I know not what I can do with him, except indeed make a Christian of him! This might induce the negroes to believe, that he has lost his infernal power by the superior virtue of the holy water, but, perhaps he may refuse to be Christened. However, I will at least ask him the question and if he consents, I will send him—and a couple of dollars—to the clergyman—for he shall not have so great a distinction as baptism from massa's own hand—and see what effect "white obeah" will have in removing the terrors of this professor of the black.[11]

The "white obeah" was no match for black obeah and so Lewis had to agree for Bessie to see a black obeah-man who lived in the mountains to alleviate her suffering.

Cynric R. Williams, who visited Jamaica in 1823, indicates that one of the tasks of Christianity was to protect the populace from obeah. The Bible became an important charm, the symbol of "white obeah," which ensured this protection for one who carried the book with him.[12]

In West Africa, the worship of the gods was organized in cult groups, often esoteric, which used drums, dancing, dreams, and spirit-seizure as part of organized worship. An aspect of this survived in Jamaica in the myal cult.[13] Perhaps the real difference between obeah and the myal cult is that whereas the obeah-man was a private practitioner, hired by his client for a specific purpose, the myal-man was a leader of a cult group, devoted to organized religious life. Like the obeah-man he tried to control the supernatural world of the shadows. Myal practices, which included ceremonies, dances, and shrines, were also designed to prevent evil spirits from doing harm to black people.

On December 21, 1781, the Jamaica Assembly passed a law calling for punishment and death to the practitioners of obeah and myalism:

> In order to prevent the many mischiefs that may here after arise from the wicked act of negroes going under the appellation of obeah men and women, pretending to have communication with the devil and other superstitions and are deluded into a belief of their having full power to exempt them whilst under protection from any evils that might otherwise happen: Be it therefore enacted under the authority aforesaid, any negroe or other slave who shall pretend to any supernatural power, and be detected in making use of any blood, feathers, parrots-beaks, dogs-teeth, broken bottles, grave dirt, rum, eggshells, or any other materials relative to the practice of obeah or witchcraft, . . . shall upon conviction before two magistrates and three freeholders, suffer death or transportation.[14]

This attempt to erase the practice of black religion did not succeed. In fact, the obeah- and myal-men assumed positions in the black community above the prestige of the ordinary black person. The myal-man and the obeah-man became persons with whom one had to deal with fear and respect. They became feared like the African priest and medicine man.

The preoccupation of black people with the spirits of their ancestors led to a special attachment for the family burial place, which became the home of the friendly spirits. Ancestral-grave dirt also became an important obeah charm to ward off unfriendly spirits.[15]

Obeah and myalism, which served as centers of the black world, were not influenced by the European world. Prior to 1830 very few black people would have been touched by Christianity. M. G. Lewis, who was an influential member of the Church of England in Savannah la Mar, Jamaica, indicates something of the attitude black people had toward the established church in Jamaica.

> The minister of Savannah la Mar has shown me a plan for the religious instruction of the negroes, which was sent to him by the ecclesiastical commissaries at Kingston. It consisted but of two points: against the first (which recommended the slaves being ordered to go to Church on a Sunday) I positively declared myself. Sunday is now absolutely the property of the negroes for their relaxation, as Saturday is for the cultivation of their grounds; and I will not suffer a single hour to be taken from them for any purpose whatever. If my slaves choose to go

to Church on Sundays, so much the better; but not one of them shall be *ordered* to do one earthly thing on Sundays, but that which he chooses himself.[16]

The slaveowner went on to point out that the minister of the established church also requested that he be allowed to visit the slaves on his estate. He gave his minister the opportunity to visit with black people but doubted if the pastor would accomplish anything worthwhile among black people in an attempt to Christianize them. The nineteenth-century established church in Jamaica was the white man's church, and so it was to remain long after emancipation. The general religious revival in Britain, which was to become a driving force behind emancipation, did not bring a large number of missionaries from the dissenting sect until the 1820s.

The Afro-Christian sects in Jamaica date from the end of the American Revolution, when several hundred American slaveowners migrated to Jamaica, taking their slaves with them. Some of these slaves were already converted to Christianity. Once in Jamaica they became unofficial missionaries. By the 1830s their teaching had spread to many different parts of the island, being transformed in the process into a combination of orthodox Christianity and black religion.[17] One of the characteristics of the Afro-Christian groups was their emphasis on "the spirits." Given the prestige of the master's God, it is understandable that Christ and John the Baptist found a place among the African pantheon.

There is a school of thought which claims that not much from the African world was carried over into Jamaica. In his book *Jamaica, Land of Wood and Water,* Fernando Henriques contends that only in folklore and magic has the African world survived. He bases his argument mainly on an analysis of the different tribes from which black people came, the different tribal languages they spoke, coupled with the extreme oppression they bore. These factors, he contends, prevented them from maintaining their original patterns of behavior. Another factor Henriques alludes to, which would prevent the maintaining of the African world in Jamaica, is the nature of slavery itself as it was practiced in Jamaica. Slaves were often separated from their tribal and communal ties and sent to other parts of the country. African family life, especially the African conception of marriage, could not survive under such conditions, as we have seen earlier.

Henriques does not take sufficiently into account the nature of common-law marriage as practiced in Jamaica. How does he explain the permanence of common-law marriage if he negates its African basis? "I've lived wit me man for twenty years and we never quarrel. We as good as them that married in Church. Sometime I tink we better." Henriques has not raised the question of how black people adapted to the situation. Indeed, the question of survival included that of adaptation.[18]

Daniel Guerin, in *The West Indies and Their Future*, argues that it was mainly the African religious customs and beliefs which survived as black people adapted to their new world, because in religion the slave posed the least threat to the master. Black religion, Guerin contends, was nurtured in the home and it was there that the mother passed it on to the children. He also calls attention to the secret societies the slaves formed, as they often met in the forests to celebrate their ancient rites. "It remains an incontrovertible historic fact," says Guerin, that "in the very teeth of white oppression, African religion was the earliest manifestation of the Caribbean peoples' racist consciousness."[19] Black religion constituted the earliest form of protest which black people could offer in the strange new world of oppression.

Given the fact that the established church was concerned mainly with the plantocracy and that only Baptists and Methodists indicated a keen interest in black people, black religion swept Jamaica. "The persecuted myal men often became Methodist preachers. . . . During slavery the myalist Methodist posed a grave problem for the planters. . . ."[20]

African traditional religion played a key role in shaping the world of black people, and hence can shed further light on the world from which black people came. It will also be important to investigate the similarities between the African world as represented in African traditional religion and the Old Testament. Perhaps the similarities between these two worlds could open the door for an authentic interpretation of black religion, which would take seriously the biblical roots of the black experience and provide a basis in the black experience for an understanding of religion and identity.

AFRICAN TRADITIONAL RELIGION

Although the world-view of the African is religious, the African's concept of self and the world was not shaped by Christianity. The Christian witness on the continent can be traced to the fourth century; yet outside Egypt and Ethiopia, it is difficult to document any serious attempt to Christianize Africa.* As we chart the pilgrimage of black people and their God in history we shall note the failure of the Christian church to shape decisively the image of humanity that emerged in these crucial years. We must now focus our attention on the role of African traditional religion and seek to discover its impact on the African theological estimate of humanity.

---

* Professor Bolaji Idowu comments on the failure of the Christian Church to influence the traditions that emerged in Africa: "There was a Church in North Africa. That Church was the mother of those great makers of Church history—Augustine, Tertullian, Cyril, Athanasius, to name a few. She is no longer in existence today: she perished long ago. And why? It is basically because she remained a foreigner and never belonged to the environment in which she lived. Was that not partly the reason for the death of the Church founded in Nigeria in the fifteenth century through the activities of the Portuguese and Spanish missionaries?" (*Towards an Indigenous Church* [London: Oxford University Press, 1965], p. 7).

Most Africans attribute the creation of the universe to God. God is the explanation of humanity's being and origin in the world. Professor J. K. Agbete describes the concrete conceptualization that Africans have of God in African traditional religion:

> From these sources we can see clearly the attributes which non-Christian and non-Moslem Africans have accorded the Supreme Being. These attributes may be classified under two categories:
> a. the external and intrinsic attributes of God
>   1. God is almighty: The world is wide but God is the master.
>   2. God is omnipresent: If you want to tell God something, tell the wind.
>   3. God is omniscient: A great being whose vision nothing can escape.
>   4. God is transcendent: Once upon a time there lived an old woman whose favorite dish was fufu. Every time she pounded fufu the pestle went against the sky which was then very near to the earth. On one occasion the sky felt so much disturbed by the old woman's pestle that it receded to its present distance from the earth. (The point is that God lives in the sky or he is the sky.)
> b. the moral attributes of God
>   1. God is a good creator. (The hawk says: Every thing created by God is good.)
>   2. God is a God of order. (God does not like disorder, therefore he has given a name to every thing.)
>   3. God is gracious. (God pounds the fufu for the armless person.)[21]

God is the source of all life, and as Supreme Being he is the epitome of all power. Humanity in all its manifestations comes from God, and from the foregoing it may be easily deduced that the point of departure for talk about the Supreme Being is people. To raise the epistemological question concerning the nature and being of God presupposes an understanding of the nature and being of people. "Every thing created by God is good." People and their God in history seem to be the theme of African traditional religion. In this world-view, God does not exist for himself, but for people.

Various stories in African traditional religion seek to explain the origin of people and their world, and many of these stories affirm God as creator. It is immaterial whether the first man and woman were created under a certain sacred tree or on a mountain or in a cave. It is also unimportant whether one person was made from brown or black clay or from ashes. Of the first importance is the fact that the person was created by God.[22]

In African traditional religion a person is usually considered to be body and soul. The Akan, in Ghana, are a good illustration of a people who hold this belief. For the Akan, a person consists of the blood of his or her mother *(monga)*, a life soul *(Kra)*, and a personality soul *(sun sum)* or, later, *ntro*.

"Because the *Kra* is the spark of divinity, each man is in direct touch with God."[23] The *Kra* is therefore pure and has a purpose to accomplish during the life of each individual. The affinity of body, soul, and spirit in the individual may be compared to a steam engine. The complete machine is the engine, but its effective performance is dependent on steam for its power and on the pistons for its movement. The steam is always pure, but if the pistons are in bad repair the steam is wasted and the engine loses potential power. However, in spite of faulty pistons and the loss of power in the engine, the steam remains pure.[24]

Many stories claim that people were originally created in a state of happiness with the gift of immortality or with the ability to rise from the dead. The first people were provided by God with all the amenities that would make them happy. They were taught by God the arts of cultivating, of cooking food, and even of making beer. According to these stories, God not only provided for the physicial needs of the people, but also for their spiritual welfare. Hence God is referred to as living with the first couple or as being a frequent visitor. "It was like a family relationship in which God was the parent and men were the children. He provided his presence among them, and all other things derived from that relationship so long as it lasted."[25]

THE DISTANCE BETWEEN PEOPLE AND THEIR GOD

African peoples lived with a sense of both the presence and the absence of God. The first people lived in a state of happiness, but they lost the happiness of paradise when a distance grew between them and God. In explaining this distance between humans and God, which results in the loss of human happiness and peace, the Ashanti claim that God, who lived in the sky, yet close to them, was obliged to recede further because of the noise of mortars pounding traditional food.[26] According to the Mende, although God once lived with his people, he left because he became tired of their gifts. Or again, stories from the White Nile tell of heaven and earth being joined by a rope or bridge, but the link was broken and so created a distance between God and human beings. This distance between God and human beings explains their unhappiness, their bondage, and the fact of death. "It is remarkable that out of these many myths concerning the primeval man and the loss of his original state, there is not a single myth, to my knowledge," writes John Mbiti, "which even attempts to suggest a solution or reversal of this great loss."[27] People accepted the separation, and in some societies God appears only in times of need or crisis.

BLACK PEOPLE AND THEIR COMMUNITY

The community provided for black people the context with which the possibility to become more fully human in history became real. Thus tremendous damage was done to the personality of the black person when he or she was forced to live outside the indigenous community. Freedom for the black person meant a situation in which the self experienced itself in harmony with the community. It was in the context of the community that the self experienced the unity of freedom and destiny. With this understanding of being-in-community, one ceased to experience a brother or a sister as the limit of one's freedom but, rather, as the possibility through which the search for identity and meaning was more fully realized. "Existence-in-relation sums up the pattern of the African way of life," Swailem Sidhom says. And this means "a vital link with nature, God, the deities, ancestors, the tribe, the clan, the extended family and himself."[28]

The first man and the first woman, in African traditional religion, were God's people, created by God. In the community they become social persons. There the individual discovers herself or himself in terms of duties, privileges, and responsibilities to self and peers. Suffering and joy have meaning only in the community. In marriage neither the wife nor the children "belong" to the nuclear family, but to the corporate whole. "Whatever happens to the individual happens to the whole group, and whatever happens to the whole group happens to the individual," writes Mbiti. "The individual can only say: 'I am, because we are; and since we are therefore I am.' This is the cardinal point in the African view of man."[29]

Because this profound sense of community characterizes African life, the various states of birth, adolescence, marriage, and death are communal events. At birth a child is given three names. The mother's family, the father's family, and the medicine man have the privilege of naming the child. The role of the medicine man is unique, because in a real sense he represents the ancestors, in that it is his task to divine which ancestor entered the child and then name the child accordingly. After the naming of the child, the families celebrate together in a sacrificial feast in which the ancestors are included by the blood of an animal offered as an oblation being given to them. In this rite the parents of the child and the ancestors are united in one community.[30]

An important feature of this corporate relationship is the demand on the individual to engage in a lifestyle that will enhance the well-being of the community. One way to achieve this is for the individual to fulfill his or her destiny in the context of the community. The Yoruba speak of this concept as *Ori*, the Ibo as *Chi*, and the Akan as *Nkraba*. In each instance, the destiny is believed to come from God.[31] For the Yoruba, this destiny of the individual either is chosen by the person, or, if the person refuses the privilege of free choice, is assigned by Oludumare, the Supreme Being. According to the Akan, at birth the child enters the world with a purpose. In both cases, there is a sense of compulsion with which one faces the task of fulfilling one's destiny in the community. If one fails to fulfill his or her destiny, the person must return through reincarnation to do so. For the Akan, sin is not a private thing that one person experiences in opposition to other people. Sin constitutes whatever threatens the unity of the community. It is in the unity of the community that a public space is created for freedom in history.

People's life in the community is governed not only by social sanctions but by God, who is, after all, their creator. No one can presume to usurp God's role in dealing with others. Because the neighbor belongs to God, one is never free to hurt the person. "If a man feels aggrieved and disposed to take revenge, he must first seek permission of God. So the Mende of Sierra Leone always invoke the name of God before uttering a curse on anybody."[32] Good or evil can come to a person only in the context of providence. When a person is successful in life, it is thought that the success was made possible because God protects the person. God is "at the person's back." The imagery here is that of the strong protecting the weak. If one escapes danger, it is because God defends him or her; and even if a person commits a crime and is not caught, it is because God is defending and protecting the person. "So the offended party is often heard to exclaim, 'O God, do not go on defending and protecting him!' "[33] For these people, both good and evil come from God, either directly or indirectly. The world is not a child of chance; it is ruled and governed by God.

THE AFRICAN WORLD AND THE OLD TESTAMENT WORLD

Another way of looking at the world from which black people came is to compare it with the Old Testament world. There are significant similarities between black people's world, as it is reflected in African traditional religion, and the Old Testament world.

Scholars and missionaries alike testify to the fact that Africans find the Old Testament easy to understand. The atmosphere of the Old Testament is like the atmosphere they breathe. Their agricultural style of life, their frank talk about offspring, their longing for offspring, and the concrete ways in which they talk about God and people, "these and many other features make this literature an appropriate vehicle of a spiritual message."[34] The stories in African folklore are so similar to the stories of the Old Testament that it makes the remembering of the Old Testament simple for black people. This is especially true of books such as Genesis, Exodus, Joshua, Judges, Ruth, Kings, and Chronicles, where narrative is the essential element.

The relationship between African and Hebrew concepts is apparent in the many parallels between African myths and Hebrew stories, from accounts of creation, sibling rivalry, and great floods, to the crossing of mighty waters. Yoruba myths, for example, depict Olodumare creating animals and plants. Also there is the concept that although Olodumare commanded the god Orisanala to mold the physical form of man out of clay, yet it was Olodumare himself who gave man life. This points to an important factual difference from the Genesis story of creation, where God made man out of clay and gave to him the gift of life. Another fundamental distinction between the Old Testament and the African world is that whereas in the African stories Olodumare communicates with Orisanala or with divinities, in the Old Testament God speaks with man (Exod. 33:11).

There is also an important distinction between the African's understanding of covenant and the Old Testament concept of covenant. The institution of the Sinaitic covenant had in it, with the concept of Lord and subject, the idea of the kingdom of God. For Israel the covenant was primarily an agreement between itself and God; this was made possible by the divine initiative. For the African world, the covenant is a human agreement in which both parties play the same role. As we have seen, the profound sense of community characterizing African life assumed the community's covenantal relationship.[35]

The comparison of African traditional religion and the Old Testament indicates a link between black religion and biblical religion. The search for freedom in history runs like a black thread through both worlds. If black religion must address with cogency the problem of identity that slavery created in Jamaica, it must take the world from which black people came seriously. To interpret a people apart from their world is to misinterpret them. It is to build a fragile bridge of self-understanding, which could not bear the weight of their history. Not only the world from which black people came, but also the world which they made, must be understood.

THE WORLD BLACK PEOPLE MADE

To examine the world black people made is to raise the prior question concerning the world that confronted them when they were forcibly brought to the New World, in chains, as beasts of burden to work on plantations. At this level we get a picture of what the world of oppression sought to make of black people. The world that confronted them was one in which an economy was built by the destruction of their bodies while the planter instructed the church to preach to their souls. It was a world in which the masters "believed that their slaves, being taught the will and commandment of the Lord, would become more submissive and obedient, would learn to serve their master faithfully as if they served their Lord. . . ."[36]

One of the great tragedies of this world that confronted black people was that of the white person wanting to be revered as God: the creature wanting to be revered as the creator. And the creature in this world of abject suffering sought to separate the bodies and the souls of black people. It was this false understanding of humanity which made the Moravian church in the Caribbean own slaves and plead with the slaves to be better slaves.[37] Because of this false understanding of humanity, "when the Spanish took over the island in 1509, it is said that the natives were 'hanged' . . . by thirteens in honor of the thirteen apostles. When the English conquered

Jamaica in 1655, Cromwell is supposed to have advised the enslavement of the negroes 'for their spiritual advantage.' "[38] The attempt to separate the unity of the experience of body and soul in the black person provided a rationale for the church to support an economic system built on the abuse of black bodies while the church sought to save their souls. The contradiction inherent in separating body and soul is apparent if one speaks of a person as "life or soul of his body," to use the words of Karl Barth.[39] This formulation, in which a person "would not be body, unless he were life or soul," calls into question the oppressive world that confronted black people in Jamaica, and sought to save their souls and destroy their bodies.

The false understanding concerning human nature, which abounded in the world of oppression, made the masters treat black people as property. Their failure to recognize that the soul belongs to "a physical and therefore material body, from which it cannot be parted,"[40] often made them demand absolute allegiance from black people. The Reverend Mr. Buchner recalls an incident:

A slaveholder does not acknowledge any other power over his slave than his own. God's commandments, convictions and conscience, he will and does, set at defiance—he laughs at them. Even after slavery had been abolished, I had once to plead the cause of a former slave against his master, who had ordered him to do what was awfully sinful. "This man," I said, "knows it and feels it to be wrong; how then can you expect him to do it?" "What," he answered, "did not I tell him? What business has he to think, or to judge, or to set up his conscience after I have commanded him!" Yes, the slaveholder demands obedience of body and soul. . . .[41]

Buchner's description of the white master's disregard for black people and of white people's demand that they be feared as God by the black populace seems to be supported by M. G. Lewis in his *Journal of a West Indian Proprietor*. Lewis, who was himself a slaveowner in Jamaica, informs us of a common practice of a slaveowner called Bedward, who would demand that any slave who had become sick and too old to work on his estate "be carried to a solitary vale upon his estate, called the Gulley, where he was thrown down, and abandoned to his fate; which fate was generally to be half devoured by the john-crows, before death had put an end to his sufferings."[42] According to planter Lewis a black person who was sent to the Gulley to be destroyed by john-crows would cry for mercy. "One poor creature, while in the act of being removed, screamed out most piteously 'that he was not dead yet'; and implored not to be left to perish in the Gulley. . . . His cries had no effect upon his master. . . ."[43] Black people who lived in this world of abject suffering expressed their prayer in a song:

Take him to the Gulley! Take him to the Gulley!
But bringee back the frock and board.
Oh! massa, massa! me no deadee yet!
Take him to the Gulley! Take him to the Gulley!
Carry him along![44]

As the black cry for help resounds in history, one cannot help asking, Where was the master's mind? Was it relaxing in the sun or asleep at church? Perhaps neither is the answer. It could be that the master understood the black person as an extension of his own will. He owned the slave and as a consequence demanded absolute obedience from the black person in life and in death. It did not occur to some masters that black people could not become totally submissive or remain perpetual children. Eugene Genovese points out the contradiction inherent in the master's attempt to demand absolute obedience from black people:

The humanity of the slave implied his action, and his action implied his will. Hegel was therefore right in arguing that slavery constituted an outrage, for in effect, it has always rested on the falsehood that one man could become an extension of another's will. If one could so transform himself, he could do it only by an act of that very will supposedly being surrendered, and he would remain so if he chose to. The clumsy attempt of the slaveholders to invoke religious sanction did not extricate them from this contradiction. The Christian tradition, from the early debates over the implications of original sin through the attempts of Hobbes and others to secularize the problem, could not rationally defend the idea of permanent and total submission rooted in a temporarily precise surrender of will. The idea of man's surrender to God cannot be equated with the idea of man's surrender to man. . . .[45]

In the world that the slaveholder made for black people, every attempt was made to reduce these people to "peoplelessness." A slave "who raised his hand by nature's instinct for his own protection, or struck, or dared to strike, or used any violence . . . was doomed to suffer death." The black person was unprotected from the tyranny of the master. If a black person was injured or maimed by another, the damages would be paid to the master who owned him. The slave was often sold in settlement for the master's debt. In the world that white people made for black people in the Caribbean, spiritual and moral values were reduced to market values. A slave who dared worship God without the master's permission would be liable for punishment if discovered.[46]

Black people often prayed for white people: "Father, forgive them, for they know not what they do," adding, "Buckra [the master] left him God in England, and devil in Jamaica stir him up to do all dis wickedness. Poor thing! Him eye blind, and him heart hard. . . ."[47] The prayer indicates that black people had begun to articulate a theological analysis of their experience of oppression. They saw the contradictions inherent in their master's talk about God, on the one hand, and their experience of injustice on the other.

Given the observation by black people that "Buckra left him God in England," we must briefly enquire whether the master's God prior to 1830 (the time by which the master/slave relationship had become institutionalized in Jamaica) was able to help black people structure their world.

The English in their occupation of Jamaica brought their church with them, and it was understood that this was the planter's church. The established church was controlled by the plantocracy. This meant that the church had to reflect the interest of the masters and not that of the slaves. With this in mind it becomes clear why "the planters, who supplied the sole support of the established Church in the Caribbean, withheld aid from the Anglican missionaries on the grounds that the democratic dogma of Christianity would prove to be a dangerous weapon in the minds of the slaves."[48] From 1655 to 1808, over a million black people were brought from Africa to Jamaica, and in 1822 there were only about twelve clergymen of the established church on the island; they had no interest in liberating black people from their bondage.[49] Was this perhaps one reason why black Jamaica contended that the master's God was left in England?

The Moravians, who arrived in Jamaica in 1754, indicate that they found the black people living in total disregard of their master's God. Instead, they were relying on black religion to help them resist the cruel world the masters had made for them. The Moravian clergyman Buchner, writing a century later, stated that after black people prayed to the God of their ancestors they would offer "the sacrifice of fowls, and other offerings at the graves of departed friends. . . . Their faith in witchcraft, or obeah, was at that time very strong."[50] We must remember that the Moravians in Jamaica had slaves and the Methodists often had the confidence of the plantocracy. It is therefore important to inquire concerning the contribution of the first black preachers to Jamaica. Did they help black Jamaica to destroy the cruel world of slavery? Did they proclaim the master's God? Or did they join in the search for freedom? The black American connection will shed light on these questions.

THE BLACK AMERICAN CONNECTION

The black American connection with black Jamaica was made in 1783 when some four hundred white families, together with their black slaves numbering about five thousand, left the United States for Jamaica because they were not in sympathy with the new republican form of government, preferring to live under British rule. Among the black people thus removed to Jamaica were George Liele and Moses Baker, both of whom were to become renowned in black religious affairs.[51] Liele was the more influential among black Jamaicans, and he was also at one time Moses Baker's pastor.

George Liele grew up in Georgia, where he was licensed to preach (about May 1775). Needless to say, his master, Henry Sharp, was unusual to allow Liele to preach.

Once in Jamaica, Liele began to preach to black people there. This first black man to preach to black people in Jamaica took as the text for his first sermon Romans 10:1: "Brethren, my heart's desire and prayer for Israel is that they might be saved." Liele compared the plight of black Jamaica to that of the children of Israel in Egypt. As a consequence of this sermon, Liele was imprisoned,[52] which suggests that this black American called into question the world that oppressed black Jamaica as he expressed the hope that black Jamaica, like Israel, would be saved.

The laws of Jamaica made it extremely difficult for George Liele to preach there on his release from prison. In 1802 a law was passed stating that if a free black person were found guilty of preaching he should be committed to prison and kept at hard labor. If the preacher were a slave, he should be put to hard labor for the first offense and whipped for every subsequent offense.[53] This law was made firmer when, in 1807, an ordinance was passed in Jamaica stating that persons not authorized by the laws of Great Britain and Jamaica could not preach to or teach the black people of Jamaica.[54] These were difficult obstacles for the black Americans to overcome.

Liele took two steps that made it possible for him to continue to preach to black Jamaicans. First, he assured the planters that he would cooperate with them by promising that black people would not use church attendance as an occasion to plan revolts or private meetings. Liele then attached a bell to the Baptist chapel in his charge. The purpose of the bell was not primarily to inform black Jamaicans what time service would commence but, rather, to inform the masters the time worship began and ended.[55] This was one way in which Liele opted to work within the system of slavery in Jamaica and so leave open the possibility for some freedom for black people. Needless to say, Liele found great favor in the eyes of the planters and, according to the Reverend Mr. Gardner, he and the other black Americans who worshiped at the church were well respected by the planters.

Second, Liele had his church prepare a covenant and, before his church adopted it, he saw that it was ratified by the legislature of Jamaica. In the preamble of the covenant the church stated: "We bind ourselves, under an affirmation, to do duty to our king, country and laws, and to see that the affixed rules are duly observed."[56]

A look at this first covenant to be adopted by a church in Jamaica provides further clues to the black American's approach to the master's God, and also helps us to understand Liele's role within the cruel world of black oppression in Jamaica. The articles below illustrate Liele's approach:

10. We hold not to the shedding of blood (Genesis IX: 6; Matt. XXVI: 51–52).
11. We are forbidden to go to law with another before the unjust, but to settle any matter we have before the saints (1 Cor. VI: 1–3).
12. We are forbidden to swear not at all (Matt. V: 33–37; Jas. V: 12).
15. We permit no slaves to join the church without first having a few lines from their owners of their good behavior (1 Peter II:13–16; 1 Thess. III:13).
16. To avoid fornication, we permit none to keep each other, except they be married according to the word of God (1 Cor. VII:2; Heb. XIII:4).
17. If a slave or servant misbehave to their owners they are to be dealt with according to the word of God (1 Tim. I:6; Eph. VI:5; 1 Peter II:18–22; Titus II:9–11).
18. If anyone of this Religion should transgress and walk disorderly, and not according to the commandments which we have received in this covenant, he will be censured according to the word of God (Luke XII:47–48).[57]

This covenant proved so successful in assuring the planters of the goodwill of black people that other black preachers at the time used it as a basis for their own teaching and preaching, among them John Gilbert, George Gibbs, James Pascall, and Moses Baker. Both George Gibbs and Moses Baker were black Americans. The fact that three black Americans were associated with this church covenant indicates the black American influence on this document, but over and beyond that, a copy of the covenant found in the library of the Baptist Mission House, London, reads: *The Covenant of the Anabaptist Church, begun in America, December 1777, and in Jamaica, December 1783.*[58] This indicates that the black church in Jamaica is connected historically with the church in North America not only through Liele, Gibbs, and Baker, but also through the church covenant. Did the church covenant originate in the Kiokee Church in Savannah, Georgia, where George Liele was baptized by a white pastor, Matthew Moore, in 1773? The answer to this question would shed light on the influence the master's concept of God in America had on black people in Jamaica. While in America, George Liele was recognized by his master, Henry Sharp, as a "good" slave. Because of this, he was allowed to instruct black people on the Sharp plantation and, later, on other plantations along the Savannah River. After receiving his license to preach, he did so in the Savannah River area until, following the outbreak of war, his British sympathies made him unacceptable as a preacher in the area.[59]

It seems quite clear that Liele, who found favor with his master in America and undoubtedly also the masters in the Kiokee Church at Savannah, was able soon after his arrival in Jamaica to make peace with the masters in Jamaica. It is clear from the covenant that his understanding of the master's God made it possible for him to live peaceably with the masters in the cruel world of black oppression. The master's God being proclaimed by a black man aroused the curiosity of the black people in Jamaica. Thomas Nicholas Swigle, a deacon in the church that Liele started in Kingston, in 1784 reports in a letter to the Baptist Missionary Society in London: "Our beloved minister by consent of the Church, appointed me deacon, schoolmaster, and his principal helper."[60] It is of interest that soon after, Swigle broke away from Liele's church and started the Second Baptist Church in Kingston. "That it was not all smooth going [in Liele's church] seems to be clear from the fact that there were several divisions in the Church. They were caused, . . . by men who were unwilling to live on the high moral level set by Liele. Perhaps the most significant group to break away for this reason were the 'native Baptists.' "[61]

The breakaway from Liele's church is very important in the story of black people and their God in Jamaica, because it focuses on two approaches to the search for freedom in Jamaica. On the one hand, Liele's contribution represents an understanding of God that was reflected in the missionaries' teaching, especially the Moravians and Methodists, and later the British Baptists. The native Baptists, on the other hand, were involved in the search for the God of their ancestors. This God represented for them freedom from the cruel world of oppression. These approaches were there before Liele arrived, but this explication of the church covenant and his request that the Baptist Missionary Society of London send Baptist missionaries to help him in Jamaica focused sharply for black people both Liele's dependence on the master's God and the inability of this God to help create a new world of freedom for black people. Was this perhaps one reason why Swigle left Liele's church to found his own?

Although Liele did not seek to free black Jamaicans from their bondage, his influence on them is attested to by an overseer who, it is reported, "said that because of Liele's work he didn't need an assistant nor did he make use of the whip, for whether he was at home or away everything was conducted as it should have been."[62]

The contribution of Moses Baker, another black American, who was baptized by George Liele in 1787, indicates that black Jamaica did not ignore the master's God. However, it seems that when Baker first arrived in Jamaica in 1783 he did not identify with Liele and his God. According to the Reverend W. J. Gardner, for four years (1783–87) Baker "lived in utter disregard of religion."[63] Unfortunately, Gardner does not inform us if Baker was practicing black religion, which could have been depicted at that time by masters as "utter disregard of religion." After Baker's baptism by Liele in 1787, he was asked by Isaac Lascelles Winn, a Quaker and slaveowner, "to instruct the slaves on his estate in religious and moral principles."[64] Baker, who by trade was a barber and had a shop in Kingston, accepted the job and went with Winn to teach black people in St. James about the master's God.[65] It is significant that when Baker went to St.

James in 1787 he found black people "living in the grossest immorality, and all firm believers in obeah."[66] Many of the slaves strenuously resisted Baker's preaching.[67] Were they perhaps unwilling to replace the God of their ancestors with the master's God? Baker also had to contend with some black leaders who had broken away from Liele's church and were seeking to make a connection between black religion and Scripture.[68]

It seems clear that the black Americans Liele and Baker, and probably George Gibbs,[69] did not seek to liberate black Jamaica from white oppression. Perhaps they could not because their teaching and preaching were based on a covenant that likely was influenced by members of the white Kiokee Baptist Church in Savannah, Georgia. This document, which reflects the master's God, was not an instrument to make it possible for black people to find freedom. The God it reflected had the interest of the slaveowners at heart.

It seems reasonable to infer that if black people in Jamaica prior to 1830 were greatly influenced by black religion, then it was not Liele's and Baker's Christianity that affected them. Most of the black people who attended Liele's and Baker's churches were black Americans themselves. Granted that there were four or five thousand Americans who went to Jamaica with Liele and Baker in 1783, it stands to reason that they may have been better prepared to identify with the black Americans and their covenant. It also seems likely that the majority of those Jamaicans who were steeped in black religion were among those who broke away from Liele and his companions and began to search for a connection between black religion and Scripture. However, the contribution of Liele went on: after his death in 1825 Baptist missionaries Knibb and Phillippo continued to teach about the God whom Liele, and Baker, represented. Black Jamaica remained interested and often sought to make a connection between the God of their ancestors and the God of the Liele covenant.

BLACK RELIGION AND THE WORLD BLACK PEOPLE MADE

In the cruel world that the master's God had sanctioned for black people in Jamaica, the black family was pressed to work hard on the plantations. Black people's working days from Monday to Friday were rigorous and tedious. They were expected to work a half day on Saturday or every other Saturday. On the free Saturday they were expected to cultivate their own garden plot. Sundays, which were often unhampered by plantation work or formal religious services, were their own. They usually spent this day at the market. The black family had limited freedom of movement. The Sunday market gave them an opportunity to meet with others from another part of the country. It also afforded black people from one plantation the opportunity for social relationships, limited though they were, with black people from other plantations.

Within this context black Jamaica was able to have relative freedom of black religion. Although the people had to work long hours in the field and had to submit to the restrictions imposed by many of the laws, and although they were expected to renounce black religion, they found many opportunities to practice a modified version of their religion within the world of slavery. In covering the form of black religion practiced by black Jamaica, we shall note especially the two periods in which black religion evolved: the first, from 1655 to 1830, when black religion flowered in Jamaica and was not greatly influenced by Christianity; the second, from 1830 to 1838, when black religion was decisively impacted by Christianity, resulting in the abolition of slavery. The second period is also crucial for the further investigations of black religion and identity in chapters 4 and 5.

In black religion as it was practiced in early Jamaica, both the myal-man and the obeah-man—usually native Africans—were able to give to the black family an impervious courage deriving from the belief that the God of their ancestors was on their side in their search for freedom. These practitioners of black religion possessed almost unlimited powers—to cause or cure disease, to bring judgment upon wrongdoers, to court or punish an enemy, to bring the dead back to life, etc. Women practiced black religion as well as men, although women practitioners were few and were usually aged and unattractive. One obeah-woman in Jamaica mentioned in the literature was about eighty years old when her white master found out about her powers. She was exiled to Cuba instead of being imprisoned, which further entrenched the belief that "Buckra could not kill obeah-[wo]man."[70]

The world in which black people in Jamaica were forced to live demanded that they find ways of expressing their understanding of the divine being on their side. The recalling of the cruel world not only indicates the oppressive context but points to the longing for freedom in history. In 1783 a slave called Mercury who lived in St. Thomas was found with ten pounds of veal in his possession. "No proof was given that he came dishonestly by it, but he had his right ear cut off; fifty lashes were inflicted at the same time, and he received fifty more twice a month for six months, and during that period was worked in chains." Again, a black woman called Priscilla ran away from the world the slaveowners made for her. She was pursued and, when caught, "both ears were cut off. She was placed in chains, and sentenced to receive thirty-nine lashes on the first Monday in each month for a whole year."[71]

The myal-man and the obeah-man in preparing black people to fight and destroy the harsh world of oppression would often administer a mixture of gunpowder, grave dirt, and human blood, which was supposed to make one indestructible. The implication of this practice was that black people believed that the world which was crushing black people was not final or permanent but that, through the power of myal and obeah, black people could find freedom in history. Edward Long, writing in 1774, notes the possibility of a resurrection experience for black people in a world in which death appeared to reign unchecked.

Not long since, some of these execrable wretches [myal-men] in Jamaica introduced the *myal dance*, and established a kind of society, into which they could [*sic*]. The lure hung out was, that every negro, initiated into the myal society, would be invulnerable by the whitemen, and although they might in appearance be slain, the obeah man could at his pleasure restore life.[72]

Writing in 1817, Matthew Lewis notes:

The Obeah ceremonies always commence with what is called, by the negroes, "the Myal dance." This is intended to remove any doubt of the chief Obeahman's supernatural powers; and in the course of it, he undertakes to show his art by killing one of the persons present, whom he pitches upon for that purpose. He sprinkles various powders over the devoted victim, blows upon him, and dances round him, obliges him to drink a liquor prepared for the occasion, and finally the sorcerer and his assistants seize him and whirl him rapidly round and round till the man loses his senses, and falls on the ground to all appearance and the belief of the spectators a perfect corpse. The chief Myalman then utters loud shrieks, rushes out of the house with wild and frantic gestures, and conceals himself in some neighbouring wood. At the end of two or three hours he returns with a large bundle of herbs, from some of which he squeezes the juice into the mouth of the dead person; with others he anoints his eyes and stains the tips of his fingers, accompanying the ceremony with a great variety of grotesque actions, and chanting all the while something between a song and a howl, while the assistants hand in hand dance slowly round them in a circle, stamping the ground loudly with their feet to keep time with the chant. A considerable time elapses before the desired effect is produced, but at length the corpse gradually recovers animation, rises from the ground perfectly recovered, and the Myal dance concludes.[73]

The myal-man seemed to have used "any means necessary" within his environment to equip his people to carve out a new world in which to live. According to Lewis, at the conclusion of the myal dance the people who needed to have their enemies revenged would apply to the myal-man for some of the same powder he had used to induce apparent death. The myal-man always gave to the people poison rather than the narcotic he used to induce the deep sleep on the participant in the myal dance. And so poisoning became one of the chief methods of fighting back which black people used to deal with the world of slavery. Lewis writes:

A neighboring gentleman, as I hear, has now three negroes in prison, all domestics, and one of them grown grey in his service, for poisoning him with corrosive sublimate; his brother was actually killed by

similar means. . . . Another agent, who appears to be in high favor
with the negroes whom he now governs was obliged to quit an estate,
from the frequent attempts to poison him. . . . It, indeed, came out
afterwards, that this crime was also affected by the abominable belief
in obeah.[74]

The white master began to fear the power of black religion. The facility
obeah gave black people "to poison to the right hand and to the left" made
black people believe that obeah had the power to make white people give
black people whatever they wanted. Black people wanted freedom. This
longing for freedom coupled with the confidence that myal and obeah gave
them explains why there was scarcely a week when black people in Jamaica
did not fight for this freedom. The longing for freedom also explains why
Montego Bay was almost destroyed by fire in 1795 and in 1831.[75]

In 1831 the last serious struggle to restrain preachers by legislative
enactment terminated, and so the church in Jamaica had a new freedom to
offer the world of black religion. Indeed, by the end of that year there was
great progress made in the number of black people who attended church
services. However, it must be borne in mind that attending church services
and becoming Christian did not mean black people had abandoned black
religion but, rather, that they were interpreting Christianity within the
matrix of black religion. Gardner makes this clear:

> Evidence of conversion and qualification for baptism was sought not
> so much in repentance and faith as in dreams; but if the applicant had
> experienced a "convence," that is, had swooned away, and while in
> that state had a vision or passed through a stage of great excitement,
> attended by physical contortion, then all was well.[76]

The Methodist and Baptist churches were able to give to black people a
new sense of meaning and power through their practice of the "class
system," which was devised to provide the means whereby an absent
missionary could be represented by a black person. Because most black
people lived in the hills, which were often inaccessible to the missionaries,
there had to be "classes" in most of these regions. In each region, there
were two or three class leaders, who virtually had the power of the missionary. The class leader was expected to know the members, to visit them, and
as the system developed he or she would take services. The leader could
also summon his or her "class," and the class was expected to be guided by
the leader.

Black Jamaica took this concept of the class leader and baptized it in
black religion; hence the class leader became a "Daddy" or a "Mammy."
Missionary William Knibb informs us of a Mammy Faith in whom black
people had tremendous confidence. They believed she had power to forgive sins.[77] It was not an accident that the rebellion of 1831, which hastened

the end of slavery, was led by "Daddy" Sharp.[78] Missionary Knibb mirrored the approach to slavery typified by the British philanthropists William Wilberforce and Thomas Fowell Buxton, who presented a resolution in the House of Commons in March 1823, "declaring that slavery was repugnant to the principles of the British Constitution and of the Christian religion, and that it ought to be gradually abolished through-out the British dominions."[79] This was the approach that good white people like Buxton and Wilberforce took toward slavery, and so when William Knibb, who was one of the important Nonconformist preachers in Jamaica during the closing years of slavery, heard that black people under the leadership of "Daddy" Sharp had taken things into their own hands, Knibb counseled them against that approach in the name of his God. Knibb addressed black people, who were ready to revolt:

I am pained—pained to the soul, at being told that many of you have agreed not to go to work any more for your owners, and I fear this is too true. I learn that some wicked persons have persuaded you that the King of England has made you free. Hear me! I love your souls and I would not tell you a lie for the whole world; I assure you that it is false, false as hell can make it. I entreat you not to believe it, but go to your work as formerly. If you have any love to Jesus Christ, to religion, to your ministers, or to those kind friends in England who have helped you to build this chapel, and who are sending a minister for you, do not be led away. God commands you to be obedient. . . .[80]

Black Jamaica under the leadership of "Daddy" Sharp disobeyed the God whom Knibb represented and responded:

We have worked enough already and will work no more; the life we live is too bad, it is the life of a dog, we won't be slaves no more, we won't lift hoe no more, we won't take flogging anymore.[81]

Missionary Knibb had to compete with the power of "Daddy" Sharp. The people refused to work, Knibb's life was threatened, and the estates were burned. Black Jamaica claimed that Knibb was bribed by white people or he would have believed "that freedom was come."

As a consequence of the revolution led by "Daddy" Sharp, missionaries Knibb and Burchell from the Baptist Church and Duncan and Barry from the Wesleyan Church sailed from Jamaica to England and presented the plight of the Jamaican people to the British Parliament.

It stands as a credit to the struggles of "Daddy" Sharp and his people that, in their refusal to "obey the command of God" through missionary Knibb, a partial freedom was granted to them on August 1, 1834. The Act Lord Stanley introduced to the British Parliament read,

> Be it enacted, that all and every person who on the first day of August, one thousand eight hundred and thirty-four, shall be in holden slavery within any such British colony as aforesaid, shall, upon and from any after the said first day of August, one thousand eight hundred and thirty-four, become and be to all intents and purposes free, and discharged of and from all manner of slavery, and shall be absolutely and forever manumitted.[82]

Yet the British went on to stipulate that a period of apprenticeship should be a condition of freedom. Persons six years of age and over were to register as apprentices and continue to work for their former owners—field hands for twelve years and domestic help for seven years. Children under six, and of course those born after passage of the Act, were free.

This gradual approach to freedom made "Daddy" Sharp challenge Knibb's assertion "God commands you to be obedient to your masters"[83] with ". . . we won't be slaves no more, we won't lift hoe no more, we won't take flogging anymore." Black Jamaica questioned the master's God and refused to be defined as apprentices. This is illustrated in a story about James Beard of Bogg Estate, who was a class leader in the Wesleyan Church. Beard was taken to court because of his refusal to comply with the law, which defined him as an apprentice. He inquired of the magistrate whether the children of Israel were apprentices when they left Egypt. Being answered in the negative, he inquired whether the magistrate would swear on the Bible that God made black people in Jamaica apprentices. Being answered in the affirmative, Beard responded, "Then God has done us injustice." Beard and others refused to comply with a law that gave them only partial freedom. They were flogged and sentenced to prison for six months.[84]

Black people resisted the system of apprenticeship and, in the first two years, "60,000 apprentices received, in the aggregate, one quarter of a million of lashes, and 50,000 other punishments by the tread-wheel, the chain-gang, and other means of legalised torture. . . ." Black people's refusal to cooperate with the masters brought the system of apprenticeship to an abrupt end on August 1, 1838, when the slaves were released. The greatest honor England ever attained was "when she proclaimed *The Slave is Free,* and established in practice what even America recognizes in theory: that all men are created equal—that they are endowed by their creator with certain unalienable rights—that among these are life, liberty, and the pursuit of happiness."[85]

J. H. Hinton provides a contemporary account of black Jamaica's celebration of the arrival of freedom.

> On the evening of the 31st, July the Baptist chapel was opened for worship, a transparency, with the word FREEDOM, having been placed over the front entrance to the chapel-yard. Of course it was

crowded. . . . After a short silence, Knibb began to speak. . . . He pointed to the face of the clock, and said, "The hour is at hand, the monster is dying." Having heard its first note, he exclaimed, "the clock is striking," and having waited for its last note, he cried out, "The monster is dead; the negroe is free." . . . During these few moments the congregation had been as still as death, and breathless with expectation; but when the last word had been spoken, they simultaneously rose, and broke into a loud and long continued burst of exultation. . . . The winds of freedom appeared to have been let loose.

The world of slavery was destroyed and black Jamaica welcomed the new world of freedom. Black Jamaica stepped onto the threshold of that new world when, on the morning of August 1, 1838, a grave was dug, and a coffin with a chain, a whip, and an iron collar was lowered into it while the people sang:

> Now, slavery we lay thy vile form in the dust,
> And buried forever, there let it remain.
> And rotted, and covered with infamy's rust,
> Be every man-whip, and fetter, and chain.

"After the ceremony, the flag of freedom, . . . was hoisted, and three more cheers were given."[86]

Black people had won a victory for freedom in which they secured the support of the church. After many centuries of using the Christian religion to justify the oppression of black people, the church at long last began to tap the liberating possibilities of Christianity. Even in the society that emerged after emancipation, the church struggled, on the one hand, with its former role as guardian of the status quo and, on the other hand, with its new identity as helper of the victims of oppression. As the story unravels, we note the attempts of black people to weave together into one fabric tenets of Christianity and of black religion.

NOTES

1. Paul Tillich, *Systematic Theology* 1 (Chicago: University of Chicago Press, 1951), p. 170.

2. See Philip D. Curtin, *Two Jamaicas* (Cambridge: Harvard University Press, 1955), pp. 23–24.

3. Ibid., p. 25.

4. Ibid., p. 26.

5. Ibid., p. 27.

6. See Howard Stroger, "Coromantine Obeah and Myalism" (unpublished

undergraduate honors thesis, Rutgers University, 1966), for details of these concepts presented here.

7. See the next section of this chapter on African traditional religion for the notion of the slaves' perception of orthodox religion.

8. Stroger, "Obeah and Myalism," p. 92.

9. Ibid., p. 96.

10. M. G. Lewis, *Journal of a West Indian Proprietor* (Boston and New York: Houghton-Mifflin Company, 1929), p. 124.

11. Ibid., p. 126.

12. See Cynric R. Williams, *A Tour through the Island of Jamaica, 1823* (London: Hunt and Clark, 1826), p. 194.

13. Philip D. Curtin, *Two Jamaicas*, p. 30.

14. Ibid., pp. 100–101.

15. Ibid., p. 31.

16. M. G. Lewis, *Journal*, pp. 120–21.

17. Howard Stroger, "Obeah and Myalism," p. 32.

18. Fernando Henriques, *Jamaica, Land of Wood and Water* (London: McGibbon S. Kee, 1957), especially pp. 23, 143–44.

19. Daniel Guerin, *The West Indies and Their Future* (London: Dennis Robson, 1961), p. 84.

20. Eugene Genovese, *Roll, Jordan, Roll* (New York: Pantheon Books, 1974), p. 173.

21. J. K. Agbete, "African Theology: What It Is," in Bethuel A. Kiplagat, ed., *Presence* (Nairobi, Kenya: World Student Christian Federation), p. 7.

22. Kwesi Dickson and Paul Ellingworth, eds., *Biblical Revelation and African Beliefs* (Maryknoll, N.Y.: Orbis Books, 1973), pp. 83–115.

23. Cited by Harry Sawyerr, "Salvation Viewed from the African Situation," in Kiplagat, ed., *Presence*, p. 17.

24. Ibid., pp. 16–22.

25. See John Mbiti, *African Religions and Philosophy* (Garden City, N.Y.: Doubleday, 1970), p. 124; quotation from p. 125.

26. Ibid., p. 125.

27. Ibid., p. 127.

28. Swailem Sidhom, "The Theological Estimate of Man," in Dickson and Ellingworth, eds., *Biblical Revelation and African Beliefs*, p. 102.

29. Mbiti, *African Religions*, p. 102.

30. Cited by Sawyerr, "Salvation," in Kiplagat, ed., *Presence*, p. 19.

31. Ibid., p. 20.

32. Harry Sawyerr, *Creative Evangelism* (London: Lutterworth Press, 1968), p. 14.

33. Ibid., p. 15.

34. Godfrey E. Phillips, *The Old Testament in the World Church* (London: Lutterworth Press, 1942), p. 7.

35. For more extended comment on similarities between African and Hebrew concepts, see, for example, Godfrey Phillips, *Old Testament in World Church*; Bengt Sundkler, *The Christian Ministry in Africa* (London: SCM Press, 1960); K. A. Dickson, "The Old Testament and African Theology," *The Ghana Bulletin of Theology* 4, no. 4 (1973). On the meaning of the Sinaitic covenant, see Walter Eichrodt, *Theology of the Old Testament*, vol. 2 (London: SCM Press, 1967), pp. 96–97.

36. J. H. Buchner, *The Moravians in Jamaica* (London: Longman, Brown & Co., 1854), p. 16.

37. Ibid., p. 20.

38. J. P. Gates, "George Liele," *The Chronicle* 6, no. 3 (1943): 122.

39. Karl Barth, *Church Dogmatics*, vol. 3, part 2 (Edinburgh: T. & T. Clark, 1968), p. 350.

40. Barth, *Dogmatics*, vol. 3, part 27, p. 351.

41. J. H. Buchner, *Moravians*, pp. 32–33.

42. M. G. Lewis, *Journal*, p. 270.

43. Ibid., p. 271.

44. Ibid., p. 270. "Frock" refers to shawl, an article of clothing, and "board" is the word for stretcher.

45. Eugene D. Genovese, *Roll, Jordan, Roll*, p. 88.

46. Rev. James M. Phillippo, *Jamaica: Its Past and Present State* (London: Unwin Brothers, 1843), pp. 158–59, 363; quotation from p. 158.

47. Ibid., p. 363.

48. Howard Stroger, "Obeah and Myalism," p. 85.

49. W. J. Gardner, *A History of Jamaica* (London: T. Fisher, 1873), pp. 244–45, 347.

50. J. H. Buchner, *Moravians*, pp. 30–31.

51. Gardner, *History*, p. 343.

52. Gates, "George Liele," *The Chronicle* 6, no. 3 (1943):124.

53. Gardner, *History,* p. 348.

54. Ibid., p. 349.

55. Gates, "George Liele," p. 124.

56. Ernest A. Payne, "Baptist Work in Jamaica before the Arrival of the Missionaries," *The Baptist Quarterly* 7 n.s. (1934–35): 24 (London, Baptist Union publication).

57. Ibid., pp. 25–26.

58. Ibid., p. 20.

59. Gates, "George Liele," p. 120.

60. Ernest Payne, "Baptist Work in Jamaica," p. 23.

61. Gates, "George Liele," p. 127.

62. Ibid., p. 128. Is it possible that Swigle left Liele's church because he had come to a similar conclusion?

63. Gardner, *History*, p. 344.

64. Ernest Payne, "Baptist Work in Jamaica," p. 22.

65. Since, according to Gardner (*History,* p. 344), Baker's instruction was based on Liele's covenant, and in 1821 many of the slaves who were taught by Baker could recite Watts's hymns, we infer that the God he taught them about was not that of their ancestors.

66. Gardner, *History*, p. 344.

67. Ernest Payne, "Baptist Work in Jamaica," p. 22.

68. Gardner, *History*, p. 344.

69. Information on George Gibbs is scant. Ernest Payne ("Baptist Work in Jamaica") says that he came from one of the southern states of America and formed his own church, which practiced "triune immersion." He died in 1826.

70. See Gardner, *History*, pp. 186–90.

71. Ibid., p. 178.

72. Cited by Howard Stroger, "Obeah and Myalism," p. 101. Long's contention

here is that the myal-men created a society in which they could practice the myal dance.

73. M. G. Lewis, *Journal*, pp. 294–95.

74. Ibid., pp. 126–27.

75. Ibid., pp. 127, 238.

76. Gardner, *History*, p. 357.

77. Ibid., p. 358.

78. In a confrontation between missionary Knibb and "Daddy" Sharp, the people followed "Daddy" Sharp.

79. James M. Phillippo, *Jamaica*, p. 162.

80. In John Howard Hinton, *Memoir of William Knibb* (London: Houlston and Stoneman, 1847), p. 118.

81. In Trevor Munroe et al., *Struggles of the Jamaican People* (Kingston: Workers' Liberation League, 1977), p. 16.

82. In Phillippo, *Jamaica*, p. 169.

83. In Trevor Munroe et al., *Jamaican People*, p. 13.

84. Robert Stewart, "Jamaican Views of God in the Nineteenth Century," in *Justice*, no. 15 (March 16, 1975), p. 9, Kingston Social Action Center publication.

85. Phillippo, *Jamaica*, pp. 171, 175.

86. Hinton, *William Knibb*, pp. 256–57.

3

Christian Hope and Freedom in History

When Jürgen Moltmann calls for an eschatological faith that does not flee the world but struggles to bring the world into conformity with the new future of God, black Christians know what he is talking about. Indeed, it would be difficult to find a better example anywhere of that combination of profound trust in the eschatological promises of God with concrete application to the political and economic realities of this world than that which characterizes the black churches in America. Perhaps it has something to do with roots in African thinking that includes the unwillingness to adopt rigid time distinctions between the past, present, and future found in conventional Western thinking.[1] Both past and future are drawn into the present in a way that makes it quite impossible to keep future reality from having its impact on the present in practical ways. As a result the projection of eschatological hopes into an indefinite future, so common in white piety, could not become predominant in the black church. When black people sang, "Swing Low, Sweet Chariot," they were referring to escape northward. "When the black slave sang, 'I looked over Jordan and what did I see, Coming for to carry me home,' they were looking over the Ohio River," James Cone remarks.[2]

This unwillingness to put asunder what God has joined together—the eschatological and the concrete historical—which characterizes the black spiritual ethos, is what has uniquely equipped the black church to undergird the long march toward freedom and equality of black people in the United States. The only institution that could give birth to and sustain the civil rights movement was the black church. Before black people went out on the streets to be beaten by cops and torn by dogs, they entered through the door of the black church to pray. It was not an accident that during the civil rights movement in Mississippi thirteen black churches were burned. The black church had become not only the symbol of hope but the agent of liberation for black people. The awareness of the presence of the despised and rejected one in its midst enabled the black church to become the inspirational source, the organizational drive, the sustaining power for a movement that might often have faltered and failed but for the conviction that Almighty God himself was committed to the struggle and would reward those who "endure to the end."

Moltmann's theology has given careful and systematic treatment to the themes that emerge out of the struggle with oppression. The critique in the final section of this chapter in no way lessens my own appreciation of the way in which Moltmann, by candidly facing the forces threatening Christian hope, has helped put the issue of oppression on the agenda of theology. Moreover, since the advent of black theology in North America and liberation theology in Latin America, the Christian church can no longer talk meaningfully about Christian hope without relating it to the struggle of oppressed people for liberation in history.

As the story of hope's vision for liberation unfolds, however, it must be kept in mind that the struggle for freedom is not waged only by a people whose skin color is black. This struggle includes *all* oppressed people, men and women, who are the victims of socioeconomic and religious domination. But the term "blackness" is an appropriate point of departure for an investigation of hope's relationship to liberation, because black people in the New World best represent hope's struggle for freedom.

Hope is more than the anticipation of liberation. It is both the motive force and the shape of human liberation. When Paul says in Colossians 1:27 that Christ is our hope, he makes for us a connection between hope and the liberation of the oppressed. When oppressed people make the connection between hope and liberation, they struggle to free themselves from bondage because "the Lord their God is in the midst of them" (Deut. 7:21). Hope, then, must become historical liberation, and this is certainly why in the New Testament hope is historically grounded in the incarnation of God, and why in order to understand hope in the black context we must first consider the concrete history that shaped the black experience.

Black people understood that, although God was not limited to history, he was present in history as their savior, friend, and hope. The God who became their liberator was one who suffered with them at the hands of the unjust oppressor. This God was a helper in times of trouble. The prayer of a slave woman illustrates something of the connection black people made between hope and liberation:

> Dear Massa Jesus, we all uns beg Ooner you come make us a call dis yere day. We is nutting but poor Etiopian women and people ain't tink much 'bout we. We ain't trust any of dem great high people for come to we Church, but do' you is de one great Massa, great too much dan massa Linkum, you ain't shame to care for we African people.
> Come to me, dear Massa Jesus. De sun, he too hot too much, de

road am dat long and boggy sandy and we ain't got no buggy for send and fetch Ooner you. But Massa, you member how you walked that hard walk up Calvary and ain't weary but tink about we all do way. We know you ain't weary for to come to we.[3]

Here Jesus is the oppressed one who, in his identification with the oppressed, brings hope in their struggle. According to black people, Jesus as the oppressed one would "make de dumb to speak," "de cripple walk," and "give de blind his sight." Jesus could make a way where there was no way.

This hope in Jesus for liberation was not only from social deprivations and a cruel world that was made for black people by the oppressors but also from the sin within. The hope for liberation was for both inner and outer transformation. And so the slaves would sing,

> O Lord, I'm hungry
> I want to be fed,
> O Lord, I'm hungry
> I want to be fed,
> O feed me, Jesus, feed me,
> Feed me all my days.
> O Lord, I'm naked
> I want to be clothed,
> O Lord, I'm naked
> I want to be clothed,
> O clothe me, Jesus, clothe me,
> Clothe me all my days.
> O Lord, I'm sinful
> I want to be saved,
> O Lord, I'm sinful
> I want to be saved,
> O save me, Jesus, save me,
> Save me all my days.[4]

Inner and outer, material and spiritual, are conjoined when appealing to the One who took on human flesh to liberate the oppressed.

THE WHITE CHURCH IN NORTH AMERICA

How did the white churches respond to the plight of black people? Most of the churches were so deeply enmeshed in the system that they were unable to pose a radical alternative to slavery as such. Instead, their efforts were twofold: toward the amelioration of the worst aspects of slavery, and toward the conversion of the slaves to Christianity. A typical example of this is found in the actions of the bishop of London, who was the spiritual head of the Church of England in Virginia. In 1696 he intervened with the crown, with the result that the royal instructions to Governor Culpeper included:

> Ye shall endeavor to get a law passed for the restraining of any inhuman severity which by ill masters or overseers may be used towards their Christian servants or slaves. And you are also, with the assistance of the Council and assembly, to find out the best means to facilitate and encourage the conversion of Negroes to the Christian religion.[5]

The English hierarchy as a whole was greatly concerned about the lack of success of the colonial church in converting black people to Christianity. In 1701, therefore, the Society for the Propagation of the Gospel in Foreign Parts was founded with the express purpose of Christianizing the slaves. But, the society complained, many masters would not permit their slaves to be baptized or to attend classes for Christian instruction. As Bishop Fleetwood said in his annual address to the society in 1710:

> I have reason to doubt, whether there be any exception of any people of ours, who cause their slaves to be baptised. What do these people think of Christ? . . . That he who came from heaven, to purchase to himself a Church with his own precious blood, should sit contented and behold with unconcern, those who profess themselves his servants, excluding from its gates those who would gladly enter if they might, and exercising no less cruelty to their souls (as far as they are able) than their bodies.[6]

In spite of the bishop's good intentions and his implicit questioning of the cruelties of the system, his words foreshadow the fateful division that was to allow even the more humane elements in the white church to minister in good conscience to the souls of black people while leaving their bodies in slavery.

Moreover, the contradictions in the system were soon evident within the society when it found itself the owner of a plantation with slaves in the Caribbean.[7]

After 1740 there was an opportunity for black people who lived on the frontier of Virginia to become a part of the evangelical movement known as the Great Awakening. From 1740, and especially after 1760, large numbers of Methodist, Baptist, Presbyterian, and other ministers began preaching in the frontier counties of Virginia. Many of these preachers welcomed slaves into the church. Black people in Virginia responded to this opportunity to attend church services. According to John Leland in his *Virginia Chronicler*:

The poor slaves under all hardships, discover as great an inclination for Christian religion as the free born do. When they engage in the service of God, they spare no pains. It is nothing strange for them to walk twenty miles on Sunday morning to meeting, and back again at night. They are remarkable for learning a tune soon, and have melodious voices. . . . They seem in general to put more confidence in their own color, than they do in whites; when they attempt to preach, they seldom fail of being very zealous; their language is broken but they understand each other, and the whites may gain their ideas.[8]

The church was able to convince many members of the plantocracy that the Christian slave was the best servant the planters could invest in. George Whitefield, certainly the most outstanding evangelist of the Great Awakening, remarked: "I challenge the whole world, to produce a single instance of the negro's being made a thorough Christian, and thereby a worse servant."[9] Whitefield was himself quite distraught at how black people were treated. "Your dogs," he said, "are caress'd and fondled at your tables; but your slaves, who are frequently styled Dogs and Beasts have not equal privilege. They are scarce permitted to pick up the crumbs which fall from their masters' tables."[10] Despite the evangelist Whitefield's aversion to the treatment of black people, he owned eight of these Christian slaves by 1747; and after 1750 he purchased many more.

Another example of the meliorative approach, which had the end effect of reinforcing slavery, was Samuel Davis, the foremost Presbyterian preacher to Christian slaves during the eighteenth century. He claimed that more than a thousand slaves attended churches under his care.[11] Davis expressed concern for their spiritual well-being but demonstrated no interest in their liberation from human bondage. He did encourage the education of the slaves. He supplied them with religious books and many were allowed to conduct their own religious services. He also published a short book, *The Duty of Christians*, which was addressed to slaveowners. He pointed out that masters should learn from St. Paul, who deemed it worthwhile for slaves and servants to labor. Davis informed slaveowners that it was to their actual advantage to Christianize the slaves because Chritianity would make black people more faithful, honest, and diligent. "A good Christian is never a bad servant, for Christianity teaches obedience."[12] Some masters responded to the book by allowing their slaves to attend church services. But Davis did not make a connection between Christian hope and freedom in history for black people.

A contrasting position was taken by the Baptist General Committee in Virginia, which in 1789 adopted a resolution that Christian slaves in Virginia should be set free. It read:

Resolved that slavery is a violent deprivation of the rights of nature, and inconsistent with a republican government; and we therefore recommend it to our brethren, to make use of every legal measure to extirpate this horrid evil from the land and pray almighty God that our honorable legislature may have it in their power to proclaim the great jubilee consistent with the principles of good policy.[13]

It must be noted, however, that the Baptist General Committee was not asking the church to participate in the liberation of the Christian slaves. The hope was expressed that "our honorable legislature may have it in their power to proclaim the great jubilee consistent with the principle of good policy." Perhaps the very structure of the Baptist Church indicated that there was not any unanimity among the churches and associations. The Baptist General Committee had no power to impose its beliefs on the churches.

What then was the impact of the Great Awakening on the Christian slaves in Virginia? We must conclude that there were still many masters in Virginia who were opposed to their slaves attending Christian worship. Indeed, "Many masters and overseers [would] well whip and torture the poor creature for going to meeting, even at night when work was done." The evangelical churches, after a short period of black conversion and religious instruction, conformed to planter opinion in the nineteenth century, with the exception of the Quakers.[14]

What of the churches in the north? Did they make the connection between hope and liberation?

By coincidence, the year 1628 marked both the founding in New Amsterdam (now New York City) of the first congregation of the Dutch Reformed Church and the first importation of black slaves into the colony. By the middle of the eighteenth century the black population in New York State was about 15 percent and in New Jersey about 7.5 percent. Black people in these colonies provided a ready-made labor force for the Dutch farmers who lived in the Hudson valley and in New Jersey's Raritan and Minisink valleys. It has been suggested that the members of the Dutch Reformed Church were among the greatest users of black slaves in New York and New Jersey. On February 6, 1792, Albert Hoogland, one of the trustees of the Jamaica, Long Island, Reformed Church, placed in the newspaper the following advertisement:

For sale cheap, for no fault but only for want of employ, a negro wench, aged thirty, who understands all kinds of country house work, with her two children, a girl aged eighteen and a boy aged six.

In 1770 the Consistory in New York accepted a black valued at forty-five pounds sterling as payment for back rent for the use of church lands.[15]

Whenever the church fails to understand that the gospel of hope is the good news of liberation, people are in danger of being treated as property.

But even in the anguish of dehumanization, black people would fight back as they hoped for liberation in a context that seemed hopeless. They would sing:

> All my troubles will soon be over with,
> Soon be over with, soon be over with,
> All my troubles will soon be over with,
> All over this world.

Or again, the slave would sing:

> I'm so glad trouble don't last always: . . .
> Hallelujah, I'm so glad trouble don't last always.[16]

According to John Lovell, Jr., who has collected these songs, the slaves were here singing either about changing the structure of slavery or removing themselves physically from the cruel world made for them by the oppressors.

Even free black people living in the north were subject to indignities. In 1786 Richard Allen and Absalom Jones renounced their association with St. George's Methodist Church in Philadelphia, where Allen had been one of the preachers, after they were ordered to move as they knelt to pray in a section of the church reserved for white people. Their response was to gather other blacks in the congregation and walk out as a body. According to the renowned black historian Lawrence Jones, the action of Richard Allen and his colleague should be seen as a protest against racism. Jones points out that in both north and south, black people did not have "equal access to the ministerial services and resources of the church. Blacks were forced to occupy so-called 'Negro-pews' (which were often painted black), or they were assigned to pews in the gallery. Frequently they were not allowed to enter the churches at all, especially in the South, and had to listen to the services at open windows and doors."[17] It was not unusual for black people to be denied access to the Lord's table by white Christians. There were times when black people had to hold their own services in the basement of the church after white people had gone home. Richard Allen ignited a flame of hope, which helped black people to discover that the only context in which they were free to hope for liberation was the community despised and rejected by white folk: the black church became the only place where black people would hear, *You are somebody*.

Having noted the failures of the white churches to see the radical implications of the gospel, it should also be pointed out that this same gospel somehow transcended the bondage in which it was held and signaled release for blacks who were in bondage. There were white radicals who taught the slaves to read the Bible. There were others who encouraged slaves to run away from their masters. The slaves were often aware of the stance adopted by Methodist and Quaker missionaries.

We have noted two approaches within the early church in America that illustrate its attitude toward Christian hope. On the one hand, the church did not make a connection between hope and liberation and hence could not offer historical liberation to the oppressed. On the other hand, some lonely voices were crying in the wilderness of oppression that there was hope in history for the oppressed. Thus the white church in North America—with the exception of these lonely voices—proclaimed a version of hope that was intended to deny black people historical liberation. What was the black response? Did black people accept this otherworldly hope and postpone liberation to the afterlife?

THE BLACK CHURCH IN NORTH AMERICA

As we have seen, white people interpreted Christianity from a white context, and black people, who related Christian hope to their African past, understood it differently.

Within the world of white master and black slave, black people began to transpose white Christianity into an African key—and no wonder a new theme appeared. There emerged a black hope, which became a symbol of protest. The black preacher wanted black people to know that they were somebody despite the fact that they lived in a world in which they were treated as property.[18]

Thus hope, as it kindled the flame of liberation, resulted in more than just revival meetings. Black people began to see that they would have to take their destinies in their own hands if they ever expected to actualize the freedom the gospel promised them. And it was to the Good Book that they looked for the assurance of victory.

> You may talk about yo' king ob Gideon,
> You may talk about yo' man ob Saul,
> Dere's none like good ole Joshua,
> At de battle ob Jerico . . .
> Up to de walls ob Jerico,
> He marched with spear in hand,
> "Go blow dem ram horns,"
> Joshua cried, "Kase de battle am in my hand."
> After the horns and trumpets blow,
> Joshua commanded de chillen to shout,
> An' de walls come tumblin' down.[19]

The white church interpreted the Bible in a way that sanctioned the status quo. But black people read the Bible in the light of a coming new order. Their religion transported them into that new order for which they sang:

Git on board, little chillen,
Git on board, little chillen,
Git on board, little chillen,
Dere's room for many a mo'.
De gospel train's a-coming
I hear it jus at han',
I hear de wheels movin',
An rumblin' thro de lan'.
De fare is cheap, an' all can go,
De rich an' poor are dere,
No second class a-board dis train
No difference in de fare
Git on board, little chillen,
Git on board, little chillen,
Git on board, little chillen,
Dere's room for many a mo'.[20]

George Liele,[21] one of the earliest black preachers in Georgia, was licensed to preach about 1775, after a trial sermon before a group of white ministers. Before escaping in 1783 with the British to Jamaica where he founded the First Baptist Church in Kingston in 1784, Liele baptized Andrew Bryan, who was to carry on his work in the United States. On January 20, 1788, Bryan became minister of the First African Baptist Church in Savannah. It is believed that both black and white people attended the Baptist meetinghouse.[22] It is understandable therefore that patrols were formed to observe the black church, and it was not long before Andrew Bryan was charged with using the gospel to foment insurrection.[23] Bryan and fifty other slaves were tortured and flogged. White people discovered that black people had made the connection between the gospel and human liberation. Slave-holding Christians began to get the message.

The mighty wind of hope blew messages of liberation in slave country. As Denmark Vesey and others planned in 1822 to initiate violent change in Charleston, South Carolina, black Methodists prayed almost every night for divine leading.[24] The black preacher Nat Turner, in Southampton, Virginia, expressed his impatience with slavery and organized his followers in a bloody revolution in 1831.

Though the Nat Turner rebellion was put down, this spirit, which insisted on concrete political liberation as the fulfillment of Christian promises, could not be defeated, and it was to reemerge in the civil rights movement of the twentieth century.

Emancipation only intensified the determination of black people never again to submit to slavery in any form.

O Freedom, O Freedom,
O Freedom, over me,

> And before I'll be a slave,
> I'll be buried in my grave,
> And go home to my Lord
> And be free.

Martin Luther King, Jr., was the classic representation of this spirit, which combined the most intense eschatological hopes for future blessedness with moral witness and political action in the present. King was, in his life and ministry, a true son and prophet of the black church whose dream for the future was informed not by starry-eyed idealism, but by the conviction that God is faithful to his promises. Concretely this meant for King that one day his children, and the children of all black people, would be judged not by the color of their skin but by the content of their character.

MOLTMANN, BLACK THEOLOGY, AND LIBERATION THEOLOGY

What does this recital of the history of the oppression of black people in the United States have to do with dialogue with Jürgen Moltmann?

On the one hand, it enables us to see why Moltmann's theology has been greeted with enthusiasm by many black theologians. Here, finally, is a white theologian who understands the gospel in a way akin to the insights granted black Christians by virtue of their long history of suffering. Moreover, Moltmann was quick to recognize the contributions of black theology. He has not only spoken out against racism, but has defended the right of black people and other oppressed peoples to pursue their goals with more aggressive means where nonviolent efforts have proved to be of no avail.[25] The resulting dialogue has been fruitful for both positions.[26] It is not surprising, therefore, that James Cone almost made a black theologian of Moltmann, so great was the congruency he saw in their positions. Moltmann, declared Cone, reinforces the black insistence that God's promise means "that the Church cannot accept the present reality of things as God's intention for humanity." To know God is to know "that the present is incongruous with the expected future." The result is a holy impatience with the world as it is.

> It is not possible to know what the world can and ought to be and still be content with excuses for the destruction of human beings. . . . Why do we behave as if the present is a fixed reality not suscepti- ble to radical change? As long as we look at the resurrection of Christ and the expected "end," we cannot reconcile ourselves to the things of the present that contradict his presence.[27]

Another exponent of black theology whose thought reveals the influence of Moltmann is Major Jones, the author of *Black Awareness: A Theology of Hope*. His response was an early application of the themes of the theology of hope to the situation of black people in America. Jones sees black awareness as grounded in a sense of positive self-worth under a God who calls upon black people to deliver themselves from bondage and their oppressors from folly. Only a powerful conviction about their identity, their mission, and their future can sustain black people in the face of inevitable opposition and discouragements.[28]

The congruencies and parallels between the concerns of Moltmann and black theology should not blind us to crucial differences between the two. Nor should we assume that Moltmann's position, taken over lock, stock, and barrel, is appropriate to the American scene. Precisely because he is a world theologian who strives to keep his categories universal, Moltmann may prevent us from seeing the theological necessities close at hand.

Latin American theologians were the first to point this out. They claim that Moltmann, in opting for the stance of "critical theory," tries to create for theology a neutral ground over and above all ideological camps.[29] According to this scheme of things, the theologian plays the role of the universal critic who, on the basis of the perfection of the kingdom of God, calls into question every concrete political movement and economic alternative. Such independence and unrelenting criticism are supposedly necessary out of loyalty to the absoluteness of the kingdom of God, lest theology be identified with—and therefore serve the purposes of—any single movement or ideology. (The shadow of the experience of the German church with Nazism, which sought to co-opt German theology for its own purposes, undoubtedly lay behind Moltmann's unwillingness to commit theology to the role of handmaid for any political cause and his insistence on a consistently critical stance.) As José Míguez Bonino insists, however, far from being genuinely universal, this critical stance is in the pattern of the European Enlightenment and results in an "idealism" that floats above the real world of concrete political and economic options, an idealism that avoids a commitment to those alternatives that are most consistent with the gospel. "There is no divine politics or economics," says Míguez Bonino, "but this means that we must resolutely use the best *human* politics and economics at our disposal."[30] God does not dwell at a critical distance either above the world or in an indefinite future; he works in and through what is available in the world and calls upon us to meet him there.

A final difficulty, inherent from a black standpoint, in a theology that locates God's being in the future is that it robs the present of the assurance of divine reality in our midst. From Moltmann's perspective, the distinction between present and future must be maintained in order that God's being (as future) not be compromised by identification with the present order. Only in this way can he be the radical alternative to this age. Black piety solves this problem, however, not by appeal to what—in the black milieu—seems unnatural and rationalistic distinctions between present and future. The black church protects the sovereignty of God by its understanding of the Spirit. The Spirit is the presence of God experienced as a palpable reality. The Spirit cannot be defined, therefore, simply as the "living remembrance'' of the crucified and risen Christ coupled with a lively hope for the kingdom.[31] Black people find it difficult to become enthusiastic about the ''delayed gratification'' that seems endemic to any Calvinist position. It is the experience of God here and now that sustains them. Their confidence in the promises of future victory in God's kingdom is based on their experience of his sovereignty as overwhelming spiritual power now. They *know* he will win the battle. In this confidence they do battle with the oppressive powers of this world.

Therefore, on the North American scene it is not enough to speak from a universal theological perspective and say that Jesus identifies with the oppressed, the *ochlos*, that great ''mass without guidance and direction, the multitude without political and spiritual meaning, . . . who have no firm community, . . . who are unorganized and lack a collective identity.''[32] This all sounds very good until one realizes that it can allow theology to remain in generalities. The pertinent fact that North American theologians must recognize, if we are not to give up the concreteness of the incarnation in the black context, is that the disinherited peoples with whom Jesus identifies are not nameless, faceless, and countryless. These people are *black*, their faces are *black*, their history is *black*! For theologians to operate in ignorance of this fact, or with indifference to it, while at the same time claiming to present universal Christian truth, would be in contradiction to the reality of the incarnation. We must not be afraid to say that God takes on specificity in the twentieth-century American cultural situation as well as in the first century.

Does this mean that we lose all ability to criticize black people or black movements? By no means. But this criticism is grounded in solidarity with them and with their cause as the point at which God is at work in one's particular corner of the globe striving for justice and righteousness. Where God is, we must be.

Therefore, I conclude that Moltmann is of inestimable assistance in helping us to clarify the biblical underpinnings and theological principles that ought to inform our theologizing today. But we would do well to go beyond his limitation of theology to the realm of universal critical principles and see that, for the sake of *all* people, God has made the black condition his own. It is here among black people that we can say most assuredly his Spirit is at work. And the black church is the open door through which all who enter can learn what it is to hope and can discover for themselves how hope liberates.

NOTES

1. Cf. John S. Mbiti, ''Eschatology,'' in Kwesi Dickson and Paul Ellingworth, eds., *Biblical Revelation and African Beliefs* (London: Lutterworth Press, 1969), pp. 159–84.

2. James H. Cone, *The Spirituals and the Blues* (New York: Seabury, 1972), p. 90.

3. In Harold A. Carter, *The Prayer Tradition of Black People* (Valley Forge, Pa.: Judson Press, 1976), p. 29.

4. James H. Cone, *The Spirituals and the Blues*, p. 51.

5. Cited by H. S. Klein, *Slavery in the Americas* (Chicago: University of Chicago Press, 1967), pp. 113–14.

6. Ibid., pp. 114–15.

7. Cf. Bryan Edwards, *The History, Civil and Commercial, of the British Colonies in the West Indies* 2 (London: printed for J. Stockdale, 1793–1801), pp. 38–39.

8. In Klein, *Slavery*, p. 120.

9. H. Shelton Smith, *In His Image, But* . . . (Durham: Duke University Press, 1972), p. 13.

10. Ibid., p. 12.

11. Westley M. Geweher, *The Great Awakening in Virginia, 1740–1790* (Durham: Duke University Press, 1930), p. 236.

12. Ibid.

13. Ibid., p. 239.

14. Klein, *Slavery*, p. 125; quotation from p. 121.

15. Cf. Gerald Francis de Jong, "The Dutch Reformed Church and Negro Slavery in Colonial America," *Church History* 40, no. 1 (March 1971): 423–36; quotation from p. 425.

16. John Lovell, Jr., *Black Song: The Forge and the Flame* (New York: Macmillan, 1972), p. 224.

17. Lawrence Jones, "Black Churches in Historical Perspective," *Christianity and Crisis* 30, no. 18 (November 2 & 16, 1970): p. 227.

18. An important contribution for black church studies is Daniel Thompson's *Sociology of the Black Experience* (Westport, Conn.: Greenwood Press, 1975).

19. John Lovell, Jr., *Black Song*, p. 229.

20. James H. Cone, *The Spirituals and the Blues*, p. 94.

21. See J. P. Gates, "George Liele," *The Chronicle* 6, no. 3 (1943): 124. See also Gayraud Wilmore, *Black Religion and Black Radicalism*, pp. 106–7; and chap. 2, pp. 41–45, above.

22. E. Franklin Frazier, *The Negro Church in America* (New York: Schocken Books, 1974), p. 30.

23. Gayraud S. Wilmore, *Black Religion and Black Radicalism* (Garden City, N.Y.: Doubleday, 1972), p. 107.

24. Ibid., p. 83.

25. Cf. Jürgen Moltmann, *Religion, Revolution and the Future* (New York: Scribner's, 1969), pp. 40f., 129ff.; *The Crucified God* (New York: Harper & Row, 1974), pp. 330f.; *The Experiment Hope*, trans. M. Douglas Meeks (Philadelphia: Fortress Press, 1975), pp. 131–57; *The Church in the Power of the Spirit* (New York: Harper & Row, 1977), pp. 182f.; *Die Zukunft der Schöpfung*, pp. 117ff.

26. Cf. "Warum schwarze Theologie?" a special issue of *Evangelische Theologie* 34, no. 1 (January 1974).

27. James H. Cone, *A Black Theology of Liberation* (Philadelphia: J. B. Lippincott, 1970), p. 245.

28. Major Jones, *Black Awareness: A Theology of Hope* (Nashville: Abingdon, 1971), p. 137.

29. Cf. Juan Luis Segundo, S. J., *The Liberation of Theology* (Maryknoll, N.Y.: Orbis Books, 1976); Rubem A. Alves, *A Theology of Human Hope* (Washington, D.C.: Corpus Books, 1969).

30. José Míguez Bonino, *Doing Theology in a Revolutionary Situation* (Philadelphia: Fortress Press, 1975), p. 149.

31. Jürgen Moltmann, *The Church in the Power of the Spirit*, p. 197.

32. Jürgen Moltmann, *The Passion for Life* (Philadelphia: Fortress Press, 1978), p. 102.

4

The Church and Black People in the Caribbean

Prior to the 1830s the church in the Caribbean did not significantly alleviate the identity problem that threatened black people. In fact, in many respects the established church compounded the problem of identity for blacks because it symbolized an institution in which slaves were not allowed to participate; the Baptist, Methodist, and Moravian churches saw their task as saving the souls of black people.

The Church of England in Jamaica excluded black people from its ministry because the church understood religion to be mainly an exercise of the intellect, which they regarded black people to be incapable of exercising. The other churches, which regarded religion mainly as a matter of the heart, sought to make the slave "Christian." The theological concern of the missionary was to save the soul of the slave, not to raise questions concerning the ordering of slave society. This theological concern was based on two assumptions: (1) if slaves were made Christians they would be more industrious; their new faith would lessen the possibility of their running away;* (2) the Christian slave would produce a more humane master, as long as the slave worked diligently, for there would be no need for the master to brutalize an industrious slave.

---

* Robert Peart, a Muslim who became a member of the Old Carmel Moravian Church in 1813, was arraigned before the magistrates to determine what effect Christianity had on black people: "To the first question, as to the instruction received, Robert replied: 'We are told to believe in God, who sees us everywhere, and in His Son Jesus Christ, and to pray to him to take us to heaven.' 'Well what more?' 'We must not tell lies.' 'What more?' 'We must not run away and rob Massa of his work.' . . . Thereupon the judges declared themselves satisfied, and let the slaves go" (Walter Hark, *The Breaking of the Dawn, 1754–1904* [Kingston: The Jamaica Moravian Church, 1904], p. 28).

The missionaries found the fact of the situation to be different on both counts. First, they discovered that they could not make the slave Christian. Black people would not give up their drumming, their African dancing, obeah, myalism, and sexual unions, which the missionaries regarded as unstable. Second, the missionaries recognized that there was a connection between higher sugar prices and more pressure on the slaves. Slavery and Christianity were not compatible.

Following the Baptist War, as the slave rebellion of 1831 in Jamaica was called by the planters, leading Baptist missionaries (Knibb, Burchell, and Phillippo) went to England to plead for governmental reform before bloodshed increased. The British government responded by creating two bishoprics in the West Indies: one for Jamaica, Honduras, and the Bahamas, and the other to include Barbados, the Windward and Leeward islands, Trinidad, and Guyana. Among the responsibilities of the bishops was the task of fostering a changed attitude on the part of the clergy toward the slaves. Indifference should give way to pious concern. The bishops were also expected to help create the context in which the British Parliament could carry out its plan for the gradual abolition of slavery, without at the same time being on a collision course with the plantocracy. And, most important, the bishops were to ensure that there would be no more rebellions by black people. The established church had a double task: to reconcile the planters to the decline of their authority over black people and, at the same time, to assure the excited slaves that the slow death of slavery had begun.[1]

It did not work out quite the way it was planned. Emancipation came like a thief in the night, in 1834, and the end of the apprenticeship system in 1838. What of the new society that was to be formed? What plans did the abolitionists have for black people?

Basically the mother country had in mind for black people the type of society known in England, with lower, middle, and upper classes, through which the industrious and ambitious might rise. The Colonial Office wanted to see mirrored in the Caribbean a rising middle class made up of mulattoes and highly literate blacks. They wanted to see black people free, thrifty, and industrious, but also respectful of the plantocracy and the middle class. They did not want to see blacks acquiring political power.[2]

THE CHURCH AS FRIEND OF THE PLANTOCRACY

The church, especially the established church, was the most appropriate institution in Jamaica to bring together ex-slave and ex-master. As a structure it could bring together all classes of people and create a sense of community. As a moral agent it could instill in black people the proper regard for authority and the importance of thrift and hard work. The task of the church as moral agent was of critical importance if the economy of the island were to be maintained. Black people had to be taught the virtues of hard work. It is perhaps at these two levels, as preserver of a harmonious community and as moral agent, that the plantocracy expected something from the church. Slavery had made the black people of Jamaica look upon work as an unpleasant form of obedience. With the necessity for obedience removed, and the black family opting for freedom rather than money,* planters had to rely on the church to equate plantation work with the moral imperative and thereby preserve a labor force for the sugar estates. The established church, which received grants from the public treasury, had a special responsibility to meet the requirements of the plantocracy.

Black people had their own expectations of the churches. They hoped to take emancipation beyond the legal revolution it represented and make of it a social revolution. As a first step, the church was able to narrow the social distance between the plantocracy and black people by teaching the latter to read and write. Literate black people could then become deacons and preachers, and these talents had an impact outside the church as well.

The churches gained a singular importance after emancipation. They were regarded as an important key to understanding the experiment in freedom. With confidence placed in them by planters and black people alike, there is a sense in which they and not the black people were the greatest beneficiaries of emancipation.

The churches regarded it as their duty to create one society out of the various antagonistic social classes. The Anglican Church, which was favored by the establishment, saw their task as a slow process of civilizing black people. It adopted a cautious approach to giving any responsibility to black people. We recall James Beard (see p. 50), a class leader in the Wesleyan Church, who asked a magistrate if he could swear by the Bible that God had made black people apprentices. When the magistrate replied in the affirmative, Beard retorted, "Then God has done us injustice." The apprenticeship method, which was condemned by Beard as unjust, characterized the Anglican approach to dealing with black people, who were allowed "to rise to the humbler positions of lay readers, catechists and, of course, school masters"[3] in a church clearly favored by the colonial administration both before and after disestablishment.

Slavery had created the problem of identity, and emancipation had not solved it. In an attempt to maintain the support of the plantocracy and at the

---

*For black people in Jamaica the ability to withdraw their work was one of the marks of their freedom. One estate, on discovering that black people would work only three days per week (as that would give them enough to live on) decided that the way to attract blacks to work more days was to increase the day's pay. With the increase in pay, however, black people worked fewer days because they wanted only enough to live on. They preferred freedom to money. The planters called them lazy.

same time gain support among blacks, the Anglican Church, after its disestablishment in Jamaica in 1870, asserted the spiritual equality of black people with white people, yet affirmed their cultural inequality with white people.[4]

Black people tried education as a means of spanning the cultural distance between Africa and Europe. Many churches in the Caribbean united on the issue of education. The founding of church schools was one way in which the church could bring its influence to bear upon the lives of black people. The problem, as black people soon discovered, was that the church schools were making no specific effort to bridge the cultural and social inequality between the blacks and the plantocracy. The content and purpose of the educational program was geared to keeping black people subordinate and inferior to the ruling class. The ruling class "demanded and obtained the undertaking that the school would not be used to affect adversely the supply of manual labour on the plantation, nor to encourage the coloured people to wish to rise too quickly up the social ladder. . . . In the Caribbean there was a growing disenchantment among the poor with the end result of schooling."[5] The ruling class were of the conviction that the right kind of education would produce the right kind of society. Education became the guarantee that the society would not change, that black people would remain at the bottom of the social and economic ladder. This awareness that education did not fulfill the expectations of emancipation for black people explains their later disaffection for education. In *The Church in the West Indies*, the Reverend A. Caldecott calls attention to black people's disappointment with the education offered them.

> At the outset there was a glow of enthusiasm on the part of the enfranchised labouring class. But it died down to a depressing extent. . . . In Jamaica the people had very largely scattered from the estate barracks to cabins on squattings. But deeper down than this lay the disappointment of some foolish but very natural expectations on the part of the simple Negroes. They had been inclined to suppose that ability to read and write would lead to immunity from agriculture labour, . . . Thus it was that in 1866, of the 286 schools in Jamaica only one was returned as in the first class, and 190 were "failures."[6]

The schools failed because black people recognized that the education they offered was intended to produce a certain kind of black person, a person reconciled to the plantation system—and this system was rejected by black people in the Caribbean. While the task of the church was to see that this goal of education was realized, the challenge confronting black people was how their new-won freedom could become the means whereby they could regain their human dignity.

THE CHURCH AS FRIEND OF BLACK PEOPLE

The church was more successful in its attempt to provide villages for the new black family after emancipation. Although the church had failed in its attempt to provide "social space" for black people through education, it had a better record in providing physical space for them to rear their families, bury their dead, and grow their crops.

The importance of the church's participation in providing space for the black family is apparent when it is recalled that land ownership had a religious significance for black people. The spirits of the departed members of the tribe or family have a crucial role in the shaping of the destiny of the community, and they are regarded as owners of the family plot. Although the people have left this temporal world, their spirits are the real owners of the family land. The living landowners are only tenants who occupy the land as a sort of trusteeship granted by the dead. So it was a crucial decision for the black family to leave the family plot, as this meant leaving the family burial ground. To leave meant to desert the departed family.[7] It was to cut off one's self from one's history. "Not to have space is not to be," declared Paul Tillich. "Thus in all realms of life striving for space is an ontological necessity. . . . Without space there is neither presence nor a present. And, conversely, the loss of space includes the loss of temporal presence, the loss of the present, the loss of being."[8]

With emancipation, black people in the Caribbean had to give up their cottages, their family plots, and seek a new space to be. Many of the ex-slaveowners were willing to sell their lands to black people, but most of them wanted to sell large units, while black people wanted merely enough space to live, to bury their dead, and to grow their crops. Here the missionary churches were helpful in providing the organization and expertise for securing large tracts of land and subdividing for the benefit of the black family.[9]

The church was appropriately situated to offer this service to the black family, since the black family had accorded to the missionaries an important role in the abolition of slavery. Because of this, in the first years after slavery the churches were crowded with the new black people. The churches seemed to have been quite unprepared for this, as they had no programs for social reorganization. Apparently they expected the social situation to remain the same, with black people basically continuing the lifestyle that belonged to the order of slavery, the only change being that they were free laborers rather than slaves.

The church, however, was forced by blacks to wrestle with the problem of helping them to find space to live. The world that black people occupied during slavery had to be demolished. It was a world handed to them by the master, a world in which they were not free to be human. In the new world that they sought to create, "to be free was to be human, and to be human was to be free.'' The new task confronting the church was not to arbitrate between master and slave, but between free people. Thus the church was forced to come to grips with its social responsibilities. The missionaries, having led black people into the promised land of freedom, had to wrestle with the implications of the freedom of faith for other freedoms. The different sects took different positions. The Wesleyan Methodists, for instance,

> who were forbidden by their standing orders to meddle in social or political questions, generally urged submissiveness and moderation on their congregations. If they intervened at all in wage disputes, they tried to do so at the consent of both parties. Somehow, helping the Negroes to buy land was not considered intervention. Therefore even the Methodists occasionally bought a moderately large run of land for resale to their people.[10]

This custom of buying land and subdividing it for black families was also followed by the Scottish missionaries. It was one way to prevent blacks from leaving the sugar estate and the church for the woods or the hills.

The Baptists of Jamaica sought to help the black family to discover not only physical space but also "social space," insisting that the rights of black people should be respected. They counseled the black family to work for a fair day's pay and they also acquired large plots of land which were subdivided for black families.[11]

During the first five years after emancipation some 150 to 200 villages were formed, totaling about 100,000 acres. The church was also instrumental in helping over 3,000 families who belonged to the Western Baptist Union in securing $96,000 during the first three and a half years after slavery, to be used for buying family plots and building their own homes.[12]

Black people responded to the churches' participation in helping to create a space for them by joining the churches. The movement from nobody to somebody was linked to the church in black minds. One inquirer for church membership is reported to have said, "Massa, me go up and down the country, and people take me for nobody. . . . Please do baptize me; I wish to die a Christian sinner, and not a heathen sinner."[13] This dependence on the church to provide the context in which one could become more fully human was not merely an individual expectation. At one service attended by over a thousand persons,

> the minister endeavoured to impress upon the multitude the words: "If the Son shall make you free, ye shall be free indeed." When allusion was made in the service to the advantages of mental and religious improvement which the Negro now possesses, the minister was agreeably interrupted by a buzz as if the whole multitude were moved with one consent to express the feelings bursting from an

overflowing heart. "Yes, Massa, thank God, we do thank the Lord for it; bless the Lord."[14]

Church membership increased greatly among the black people of Jamaica. Membership in the Methodist churches nearly doubled between 1831 and 1841; Baptists grew from 10,000 to 34,000 during the same period.[15] With this success in membership and the large attendance of black people at worship services, it is understandable that church leaders assumed black religion to be obliterated. They regarded the influx of black members in their churches as a sign that Christianity had at long last won the day, the era of Christian freedom had come, and the long night of black religion and unchristian practices was ended. "The revelries attending births and deaths have given place to the decencies and proprieties of Christian life," declared one church leader. "Licentiousness and discord have been displaced by the sanctity of matrimony, and the harmony and comforts of the domestic circle. Revolting and degrading superstition has vanished before the light and influence of truth as 'mists before the rising sun.' "[16]

During the first decade after emancipation, something of a spiritual transformation had occurred, or so the missionary church believed. Missionaries reported that "cunning, craft, and suspicion—those dark passions and savage dispositions before described as characteristic of the Negro . . . are now giving place to a noble, manly, and independent, yet patient and submissive spirit."[17]

Apparently many of the missionary churches had viewed black people as a slate that they could wipe clean of the last vestiges of black religion. Black people's attendance at the missionary churches seemed to them to mean that this had in fact happened. Had they looked closely at what was happening in the Baptist churches in Jamaica, they would have noted that black people had not relinquished black religion, but were in fact allowing the practice of Christianity to coexist with African religious beliefs. Black people were placed between two religious worlds: Christianity as it was represented by the missionaries, and black religion as it was adapted to the black situation. The problem for black people was not merely a matter of choosing between these two faiths. In Christianity they were confronted with a religion in which they would not be assimilated and in black religion they found religious beliefs that they would not abandon even if they did choose Christianity. The missionaries mistook church attendance to mean assimilation, and they failed to recognize that black people could not abandon black religion.

The Baptist Church in Jamaica during the first decade after emancipation illustrates a context in which black people could deal with these two religious worlds. The Baptists had a system that particularly appealed to the black family, called the ticket-and-leader system. It was the practice of dividing the congregation into classes, with each class representing a regional area. For every class there was a leader, and every member had a ticket that showed membership. The ticket-and-leader system appealed to the black family because the leader of the class was a member of the black family, who had the power to call class meetings, to visit the class members, to reprimand, and to preach. The system also appealed to the black family because the ticket became a charm, which each member carried for protection from evil spirits. The ticket was a symbol representing the Spirit of the master's God.*

In addition to providing a context in which black people could deal with both the Christian religion and black religious practices, the Baptists further won the admiration of black people in that they called on the plantocracy to mete out social justice to the black family. "So long as they [the Baptists] continued to believe that compromise with the planters was only a 'false and heartless truce, which is called peace by the slaveholding spirit, but fundamentally is outrageous war against God and human happiness,' they enjoyed special position among the Negroes."[18]

The Baptists tolerated the growth of black religious practices. They gave practical advice to the black family on the question of wages, and pleaded with the plantocracy for social justice. They were also, along with other churches, instrumental in procuring lands and setting up villages for black families. They even tried to organize a political party (known as the Anti-State Church Convention), to express the interests of the villagers, "and if it had secured victory at the polls in 1844, it would have amounted to a political revolution."[19]

It was no accident, then, that black people thronged to the Baptist Church. That church, after emancipation, sought to create physical and social space for black people to be.

The other missionary churches were disturbed by the phenomenal growth the Baptist churches experienced and by their making room for black people to practice black religion. The Presbyterian and Congregational missions charged the Baptists with tolerating black religion. They claimed that the Baptists had given too much power to the class leaders, who required of their members special dreams and seizure by "the spirit" as a qualification for baptism and who had made baptism by immersion into a superstitious rite. The official Baptists had become more like the native Baptist Church before emancipation.[20] In 1843 the Jamaican Baptists severed their connection with the Baptist Missionary Society in London and became a Jamaican church. At the same time they founded Calabar College for the training of native ministers.[21]

The membership of the Methodist Church began to complain that there were not enough black preachers in the Methodist Church. This discontent

*The ticket-and-leader system is still practiced in many churches. The class leaders still have the same authority, but the tickets have ceased to be regarded as charms able to drive away evil spirits.

among the black members occasioned a split in the church, led by Edward Jordan.

These divisions in Baptist and Methodist churches indicate that blackness had become an important point of departure for black people's understanding of their world. They had not surrendered their blackness, nor had they abandoned African religious beliefs.

THE CHURCH AND THE BLACK EXPERIENCE

After emancipation the churches had too readily assumed that the black people were assimilated by Christianity, "that African superstitions had been rooted out, and that the people's way of thinking and feeling had become Christian."[22] There was, in fact, a strong revival of black religion in Jamaica in 1842. Hark describes the situation:

Around the congregation at Irwin Hill the outbreak was extremely violent and the temptation great. There some old Africans had never ceased to practice obeah, and had found it to be a very paying business indeed, for the people would not relinquish their belief in its reality. The practice was to bury, at the gate or in the residence of the person who was to be dealt with, a box or cloth, containing earth from a grave, feathers of a fowl, and other articles which in their belief would produce sickness and death, or an entire change of mind. Another class of sorcerers were the myalmen. These pretended to have still greater powers, and were accounted good and holy. They pretended to make obeahism of no effect; that they could discover and destroy it; and maintained that they were sent by the great God to purge the world from all wickedness, and that they had received power to procure rest for the wandering spirits, or "shadows," as they were called. These laid claim to immediate intercourse with God, and divine revelations; whilst their proceedings were accompanied by songs in which the name Christ, the Holy Spirit, Father Abraham, etc., were most irreverently interspersed.[23]

Although the mission churches in Jamaica were able to boast of an influx of black members after 1838, between 1842 and 1845 they lost up to half the amount of members they had gained. Philip Curtin suggests that the further black people went from slavery the more difficult it became for them to understand the mission church as the area within which they could find their identity.[24] Black people began to associate the work of the mission church with slavery, and found it increasingly difficult to identify with this church. To them the main role of the mission church was that of setting them free within the context of slavery. The distance between black religion and missionary teaching became increasingly difficult to bridge after 1842.

The missionaries had to compete with the African cults. In order for mission churches to keep their black members they had to provide spiritual satisfaction as well as social gain. The African cults were able to wrestle with the mission churches' teaching and African beliefs in a way that took cognizance of both realities. In bringing together the African religious perspective and the Christian perspective as taught by the missionary, the African cults gave to black people a reinterpretation of Christianity, which took their search for a fuller freedom seriously. The African cults gave to black people an Afro-Christian perspective, which brought about a merging of sorts of black religion and Christianity.

During this period the growth of Afro-Christian cults surpassed that of the missionary churches. By 1860 half the churches in Kingston were black Baptists. It would be safe to assume that throughout Jamaica during the latter half of the nineteenth century, the native form of Christianity had a firmer hold than European orthodoxy.[25]

Two interpretations of Christianity developed in Jamaica during this period: a black interpretation and a European interpretation. Europe and Africa were competing for black people's loyalty. This phenomenon was decisive for the development of black identity and self-understanding among black Jamaicans.

The missionary churches, competing with the native interpretation of Christianity, appealed to black people to remember the help from the churches during slavery. A missionary warned:

> . . . let the people of Jamaica be admonished if ever they should forget the God who broke the oppressive yoke of slavery; if ever they should forget their obligations to the men who for so many years endured so much reproach and suffering for their best interests; then indolence and wretchedness will be the result; the Island will be the grave of its own prosperity and will exhibit a warning to others, the melancholy spectacle of the degradation of an ungrateful people and the sin of such as apostatize from God.[26]

The mission church never regained the ground it lost. It is not surprising, in view of their continued attack on the customs and practices of black religion. The missionaries

> attacked concubinage, drumming, dancing, the Christmas festival and Sabbath breaking. This practically covered the field of Negro amusements and immoral behaviour in one of these respects was grounds for expulsion from the church. The establishment was especially strict in respect to marriage and discouraged baptism of illegitimate children. This meant in practice that at least 70 per cent of the population was barred from the church. In spite of decades of mis-

sionary training, Jamaicans would not get married. Young women felt
that marriage was a form of slavery.[27]

European marriage customs were completely rejected by black people,
and this, perhaps above all other factors, was a source of disappointment
for European church people. How would they handle the widespread
unstable unions and the high rate of illegitimacy?

At a time when sexual attitudes in England were passing from the
laxity of the Regency period to the puritanism of the Victorian ethic, it
was an embarrassment for the churchmen to report that the Negro
was defaulting in this cardinal area. As the century wore on, Victorian
cultural arrogance increased and they came to regard these people
whose sexual practices deviated from their own as suffering from
deep cultural defects which would take a long time to remove.[28]

The middle-class European community in Jamaica regarded these African traits as unmistakable signs that black people were children of nature,
and that the task of church and school was to efface these flaws in the black
family character. The church devoted the remainder of the nineteenth
century to correcting the moral impediment in the lives of black people.

Black people were to be dissuaded from their marriage customs and from
the practices of black religion. After emancipation, drumming and shell
blowing were outlawed. In 1841 two black people were killed following an
attempt to suppress the black interpretation of Christmas. The missionaries' opposition to this important festival of black people was basic to
the distrust that black Jamaica had for the mission church. Two important
consequences were (1) black people who remained in the mission churches
began insisting that they have ministers of their own color, and (2) there
was a continual loss in black membership in the mission churches as many
class leaders left to form new cults. Black ministers, apparently, could be
trusted to understand the importance of black religion as the context in
which black people would be free to become more fully human. Jamaican
Baptists did try to train a native ministry, but the attempt was only partly
successful because many ministers left the official Baptist Church to start
new cults.[29]

With the strict control of black people's social life eased after slavery,
these cults were able to involve black people in black religion. There were
notable revivals of black religion in Jamaica in 1841, 1842, 1846, 1852, and
1857–60. The main focus of these revivals was myalism. In *The Breaking of
the Dawn* Walter Hark describes a myal service:

As soon as darkness set in they assembled in large crowds in open
pastures, most frequently under huge cotton trees, which they wor-
shipped and counted sacred; and after sacrificing some fowls, the

leader began his song in a wild strain, which was answered in chorus; then followed the dance, growing wilder and wilder until those who participated were in a state of mad excitement. Some would perform incredible evolutions while in this state, until, utterly exhausted, they fell senseless to the ground, when every word they uttered was received as divine revelation.[30]

At other times there were dances for the departed, when food was placed on the graves.

> Drumming, blowing of the conches, dancing—Verily, this is more like Heathen Africa than Christian Jamaica. . . . People would meet to read the Bible; none of them could read, but they hired a man to do it for them; they listened attentively; they endeavoured to remember what they heard; one of them offered prayer in the usual way; then the leader would call: "Now let the Spirit speak!" And what a scene followed! . . . They became excited; they howled, and screamed, and fell into convulsions. . . . [31]

Although slavery had created the identity problem for black people, it did not completely destroy their cultural heritage. The missionaries had mistakenly thought that Christian instruction would erase black belief and replace it with "pure" Christianity. It was difficult for the missionary to respect black religion as a basis for an understanding of Christianity. Hence black people had to break away from the mission churches and create their own cults in which the forms and rhythms of Africa could find expression. Although a great deal of their language was colored by Christian phrases and Christian hymns, and the Bible was used, black people's spiritual concerns were historically derived from the black experience. This spiritual heritage had seen them through the trauma of slavery, and they were not willing to give it up in a post-emancipation society.

The mission churches launched a united assault against black religion in Jamaica in the early 1860s. This took the form of a revival, which was aimed to convert black people from their "heathen" ways to "pure" Christianity. The revival was a great success in terms of the number of black people who attended. There were fasting and praying, and the high point came when the Baptists set aside the last Sunday of April 1860 for God's arrival in Jamaica. There is no mistaking what had happened—the revival had turned African. The new convert was usually struck prostrate on the floor, and as the revival proceeded the black converts were given to oral confessions, trances, dreams, "prophesying," spirit seizure, wild dancing, and mysterious sexual doings. The revival became increasingly a mixture of myalism and Christianity, ending in a permanent addition to the Afro-Christian cults, and leaving the missionary churches at their lowest ebb.[32]

The "people's religion" had been formed between the poles of African and European belief. Revivalism was closer to the African pole. Christianity was reinterpreted in the light of West African religion. Black people who had received substantial instruction by the missionaries tended to lean toward the European pole.

Revivalism, however, did not answer the problem of identity that slavery had caused. The frustrations of adjusting to a new society persisted. With religion not fully meeting the needs of black Jamaica, in 1865 black people tried rebellion.

Robert Gordon, the first black man to be ordained in Jamaica by the Church of England, indicates that had the church become black, rebellion would not have had to replace religion as a method of liberation. Gordon was prevented by the bishop of Jamaica from serving a local congregation. Gordon, in a tract entitled *The Jamaica Church—Why It Has Failed*, addressed to the secretary of state for the colony, argues against the antiblack policy of the established church.

I hold that the Anglo-Saxon race having, during many generations, used their superior knowledge and physical power in injuring, oppressing, and degrading the black race, it is their moral duty to do everything in their power—now that slavery has been abolished in the countries which their "auri sacra Fames" had caused to have been its miserable strongholds—to assist in elevating them to whatever stations in life they may have all the qualifications for feeling with honour to themselves and advantage to society; at any rate, to place no insuperable barrier in their way, on the ground of colour. . . . The hateful policy of the Jamaica church, persistently carried out by the Bishop of Kingston, has ever been to make an invidious distinction between the white and coloured subjects of Her Majesty.[33]

According to Gordon, had the church become black it would have removed the contempt for blackness that was a source of division in Caribbean society: "The specific burden on the church . . . is the paying of the moral debt which is owed by the entire English nation for the crimes committed against Africa and her descendants."[34]

Gordon has touched a vital nerve in the church's relationship with black people in the Caribbean. With rare exceptions, the church did not take the history of blackness seriously. It continued to interpret black people mainly in the light of European Christian ideals.

THE CHURCH AS BEARER OF IDENTITY

We have noted the church's response to the black presence in the nineteenth century; we must now focus specifically on its response to this presence in the twentieth century. It is not possible to give here an exhaustive account of the church's responsibility to black Jamaica, but an accurate indication can be given of the church's interpretation of ministry to black Jamaica in the twentieth century.

In 1941 the Jamaica Council of Churches was formed; it included "representatives of ten branches of the Christian Church, Anglican, Baptist, Presbyterian, Congregational, Methodist, Moravian, Disciples of Christ, Church of God, Salvation Army and the Society of Friends."[35] In 1950 the council published *Christ for Jamaica*, in which the church's mission in modern Jamaica was reflected upon by Jamaican theologians. The Reverend John Poxon points out in the preface that in the first decades of the twentieth century the churches in Jamaica were aware of the intense desire for a new humanity in the "new Jamaica." The problem confronting the church was not the failure to recognize the identity problem, but to identify the method by which the new humanity in Jamaica could be achieved. One thing is clear, says the editor, namely, the answer to the problem of humanity is summed up in the words "Christ for Jamaica."

Although Poxon did not explain how Jesus Christ would be the answer to the problem of identity in Jamaica, a number of the denominations through their spokespersons sought to make the connection between the "new Jamaica" and Jesus Christ.

Speaking for the Baptists of Jamaica, the Reverend E. A. Brown said that the Baptists saw their task in the creation of a new Jamaica as that of bringing the truths of Scripture to bear upon the issues and destiny of the people of Jamaica. The truths of Scripture show that human beings, who were created in the image of God, have defaced God's image through sin, but Jesus Christ opens up a new possibility for humankind to have fellowship with God as black Jamaica recaptures its destiny. Sin has set up the distance between black Jamaica and the fulfillment of its destiny. Christ enables Jamaica to fulfill its destiny as he removes sin. Sin, for E. A. Brown, seems to be whatever separates Jamaica from fulfilling its destiny.

Brown regards it as significant that the first Baptist preacher to black Jamaica was a black person. As he sees it, the Baptists provided the first black prophets to black Jamaica, who proclaimed "the gospel to the poor, healed the broken hearted, preached deliverance to the captives, the recovery of sight to the blind, liberty to them that were bruised. . . ."[36] The model of ministry in Jamaica for the Baptists seems to be the black prophets who will proclaim "the centrality of the cross, the converted church, the priesthood of all believers, the baptism of believers by immersion, leading as they do to the inevitable demand for a social order where every man shall be treated as a child of God."[37]

Speaking for the Methodist Church in Jamaica, the Reverend Walter Richards called attention to the place of experience in the life of the individual. "The Methodist Church owes its origin to an experience and probably because of that places great importance on a living experience of

God's presence in the life of the believer.'' The main teaching is that the Christian can know that "his sins are forgiven through repentance and by faith in Jesus Christ and that he is a child of God."[38]

The Church of England in Jamaica was by this time called "the Jamaica Church." Speaking for "the Jamaica Church" was the Reverend W. J. Clarke. The crucial witness of the church in Jamaica is to announce that God does not merely exist, but that he has made himself known to people. The hope of Jamaica is in Christ, and "to say that Christ saves is to say that God saves. Our certain knowledge is that God, by his mighty act, has visited the world and by his life, suffering, death, resurrection, and all that followed these events, has opened a way out of our human tragedy."[39]

In *Christ for Jamaica* each denomination attempts to demonstrate that Jesus Christ is the answer to the problem of identity in Jamaica. The churches, though still largely influenced by European ideals of salvation, do suggest in their talk about black humanity the need for a new social order. The church's call for black prophets in Jamaica is an attempt to wrestle with the theological significance of blackness for Jamaica. At last the church has ceased to ignore the black experience. Black Jamaicans continue to experience the pull toward Africa and Europe.

In his contribution to *Christ for Jamaica*, entitled "Worship and Fellowship in the Church," the Reverend Herbert Cook supports the need for the churches to speak with specificity to the identity problem of black people: (a) if the church takes black people seriously, its ministry must meet the needs of its neighborhood; (b) the church's interpretation of the gospel must address black people in a way that allows them to understand the gospel as relevant to their present situation. Out of the history of the people, the religious genius of the people, and their categories and symbols, must emerge. As the church listens to the people, the church discovers "again and again that genius speaks in the songs they made; in ringing declarations of faith, in thunderous commands, or in the clear longing for deliverance murmuring with all the gentleness of a cradle song: Swing low, Sweet Chariot,/Coming for to carry me home."[40]

As the church reflects on the black experience, Cook says, it discovers in the people's songs and poetry their sense of the presence of God. The church encounters the black experience in "the big wheel moved by Faith."

> I know moon rise, I know star rise
> I lay this body down
> I walk in moon light,
> I walk in star light
> To lay this body, here, down.[41]

Moon rise and star rise are theological symbols pointing to the time of rest that belongs to the people of God. The challenge that confronted the church in the first decades of the twentieth century was to give the church back to the people and thereby establish a church *of* the people. S. E. Carter, archbishop of the Roman Catholic Church in Jamaica, supports the need for the church to become an incarnation of a people's quest for identity. Theology, he says, should not be divorced from black people's quest for identity.[42]

In 1973 an epoch-making book, *Troubling of the Waters,* was published by the Caribbean Conference of Churches. It called upon the churches to take the history, geography, and culture of the people seriously, as the church engaged in talk about the new humanity in the Caribbean. Horace Russell, writing from Jamaica, says that the church must concern itself with *(a)* God, *(b)* humanity, and *(c)* cosmos. Russell thinks the church in the Caribbean has attempted to deal with God and humanity but it has ignored the *world* of the people. Theology must take geography and history seriously:

> What is strange is that this positive approach to the nature of the World (Cosmos) it would appear is biblical. The biblical writers observe that there was the *hill* of Zion, the *city* of Jerusalem, the *river* Jordan, the *land* of Palestine. In the New Testament it would appear that emphasis upon a *hill* outside the Jerusalem city wall, a *stone* sealing the tomb and a *garden* of the resurrection was deliberate. There is little doubt that the world (Cosmos) in the sense being used here, God's creation, finds its way positively into the theology of the biblical writers.[43]

Theology must not ignore the world in which people struggle for meaning. Theology in the Caribbean must be approached via sociology and history rather than philosophy. As the church in the Caribbean wrestles with the issues of race, laziness, authority, the "cunning" black person, the church will come to understand through the sociological and historical method that these characteristics were indispensable tools for the survival of black people. "Similarly, the Calypso mentality—an attitude of total enjoyment and abandonment to life and the expectation that all needs will be freely granted—in many cases releases mental stress and strain where life is unbearable."[44] As the church takes modern blacks seriously, it will see in their attitude of "laziness" the judgment of God on the image of human beings as producer, production agent, and salesperson.

Dr. Watty, a Methodist minister who contributes to *Troubling of the Waters* from the United Theological Colleges of the West Indies, pleads for theology to be given back to the people, as the church's talk about God arises out of the indigenous community. "It is the beginning of the end of colonialism when the colonists ask whether 'So' is necessarily so. . . . A dog wags his tail when I throw him his bone, build him his kennel or pat his head for the stick he has retrieved. It takes a man to tell his would-be benefactor to go to hell with bone and kennel and stick."[45] Some people argue, Watty continues, that theology in the Caribbean need not be "decolonized" because theology is timeless and not historical. According to Watty, the eternal dimension of theology does not negate its historical incarnation. Theology, which is talk about God and people, should not be an import; it must arise from the native soil, as talk about God is rooted in talk about people. "Pure theology, therefore, is an ideal which does not exist. There are inevitably historical, sociological and cultural conditions which not only mediate but decisively affect how some speak and what others hear and understand about 'God.' " The incarnation once and for all proved that "christology is meaningless theologically until it is meaningful historically."[46]

As the church in the Caribbean decolonizes theology, it must be willing to put aside a timeless, universal, metaphysical theology and become existential as it seeks to relate to the living history of blackness. This is consistent with the biblical revelation, which took on historical particularity in the exodus and in the incarnation. "Theology reflects not only what men hold to be true, but even more the situation out of which they speak."[47]

The church in the last quarter of the twentieth century in the Caribbean shows evidence of a willingness to change so that the humanity of black people will be redeemed. In the eighteenth and nineteenth centuries the church in Jamaica was largely divorced from the cultural forms and patterns of the people it represented. It was a church *for* the people but not *of* the people. Because of its withdrawal from the people, it became a meaningless sect on the periphery of society and could do little for the people. The church, in its concern for maintaining its European identity, could not meaningfully minister to people with black identity. In attempting to preserve its own identity the church accentuated the identity problem of black people. Insofar as the church is willing to lose itself, it may find itself—and become the agent of salvation for black people.

NOTES

1. Lilith M. Haynes, ed., *Fambli* (Georgetown, Guyana: CADEC, 1971), pp. 27–28.

2. Ibid., pp. 29–30.

3. Ibid., p. 35.

4. Ibid., p. 36.

5. David I. Mitchell, ed., *With Eyes Wide Open* (Barbados: CADEC, 1973), p. 143.

6. A. Caldecott, *The Church in the West Indies* (London: Frank Cass & Co., 1898; reprinted Totowa, N.J., 1970), p. 113.

7. Howard Stroger, "Coromantine Obeah and Myalism" (unpublished undergraduate honors thesis, Rutgers University, 1966), p. 29.

8. Paul Tillich, *Systematic Theology* 1 (Chicago: Chicago University Press, 1951), pp. 194–95.

9. Philip Curtin, *Two Jamaicas* (Cambridge: Harvard University Press, 1955), p. 114.

10. Ibid., p. 115.

11. William Lou Mathison, *British Slave Emancipation* (New York: Octagon Books, 1967), p. 64.

12. Ibid., p. 69.

13. J. H. Buchner, *The Moravians in Jamaica* (London: Brown & Co., 1854), p. 119.

14. Ibid., p. 124.

15. Philip Curtin, *Two Jamaicas*, p. 162.

16. Ibid.

17. Ibid., p. 163.

18. Curtin, *Two Jamaicas*, p. 164.

19. Haynes, ed., *Fambli*, p. 37.

20. Curtin, *Two Jamaicas*, p. 165.

21. Samuel and Edith Hurwitz, *Jamaica, a Historical Portrait* (New York: Praeger, 1971), p. 130. I attended Calabar College from 1960 to 1964. N.L.E.

22. Walter Hark, *Breaking of the Dawn*, p. 88.

23. Ibid., p. 89.

24. Curtin, *Two Jamaicas*, p. 168.

25. Cf. ibid.

26. Ibid., pp. 171–72.

27. Ibid., p. 169.

28. Haynes, ed., *Fambli*, p. 40.

29. Curtin, *Two Jamaicas*, p. 169.

30. Walter Hark, *Breaking of the Dawn*, p. 90.

31. Ibid., pp. 92–93.

32. Curtin, *Two Jamaicas*, pp. 171–72.

33. In *Justice*, no. 9 (1973), p. 9 (publication of Social Action Center, Kingston, Jamaica).

34. Ibid., p. 10.

35. John Poxon, "The Jamaica Christian Council," in J. A. Crabb, ed., *Christ for Jamaica* (Kingston, Jamaica: Pioneer Press, 1950), p. 9.

36. Ibid., p. 18.

37. Ibid., p. 19.

38. Ibid., pp. 8–10.

39. Ibid., p. 53.

40. Ibid., p. 55.

41. Ibid., p. 56.

42. Idris Hamid, ed., *Troubling of the Waters* (San Fernando, Trinidad: Rahaman Printery, 1973), p. 4.

43. Horace Russell, "The Challenge of Theological Reflection in the Caribbean Today," in ibid., p. 27.

44. Ibid., p. 30.

45. William Watty, "The De-Colonization of Theology," in ibid., p. 52.

46. Ibid., p. 54.

47. Ibid., p. 55.

5

Black Theology and
the Black Church

As the end of an era in which black theology flowered as a full-fledged theology approaches, it is appropriate to look back on its major emphases and also to look forward to what may be its focus and direction in the last part of the twentieth century.

Although black theology in its present form became widely recognized through the writings of scholars such as James Cone, Major Jones, and Deotis Roberts, it must not be thought that black theology began in the late 1960s or early 1970s; rather, its roots are found in the attempts of generations of black people to understand themselves and their environment from a Christian perspective. In the period of slavery, these roots are in folklore, sermons, songs, and speeches. The raw material would not be formal theological reflection but, similar to the Hebrew Scriptures, God's history with his people in struggle. To affirm this connection between Israel and black people is to begin to understand that the black church was both cradle and context of black people's attempt to understand their world and themselves.

Whether one examines the contributions of George Liele or Andrew Bryan at the Yamacraw Baptist Church in 1777 or that of Absalom Jones and Richard Allen at Bethel Methodist Church in 1787, it becomes evident that the attempt by black people to relate God to the black experience in a way that called into question the forces of oppression and signaled release for victims was always a characteristic of black life in the New World.

This is illustrated in the understanding that Martin Delaney had about God and his relationship to the cruel world of oppression that victimized black people. Writing in 1852, Delaney stated that he found it contradictory that the God of the Bible would make white people prosper and curse black people. Although he saw no easy answers to the questions raised concerning black power and black destiny, he felt that black people should do more than pray; they should apply themselves in ways that would result in the changing of the world. Delaney wrote:

We are no longer slaves, believing any interpretation that our oppressors may give the word of God, for the purpose of deluding us to the more easy subjugation; but freemen, comprising some of the first minds of intelligence and rudimental qualifications, in the country. What then is the remedy, for our degradation and oppression? This appears now to be the only remaining question—the means of successful elevation in this our native land. This depends entirely upon the application of the means of elevation.[1]

Delaney was convinced that the hope for black people lay in their helping themselves and refusing to allow white people to interpret the Scriptures and the world for them. When black people read the Scriptures in the light of their situation, said Delaney, they discover that their quest for human dignity and freedom is consistent with the biblical theme of freedom. Implicit in Delaney's attempt to relate an exegesis of Scripture and society is an outline for black theology.

GOD AND BLACKNESS

Other black theologians of the nineteenth century, such as Bishop Henry McNeil Turner and Marcus Garvey, further serve to remind us that the roots of black theology are in the black church. The concept of the blackness of God, which appeared in black theology in the 1960s and 1970s, was being discussed more than a century earlier in the black church. Indeed, Bishop Henry McNeil Turner, who was elected bishop of the African Methodist Church in 1880, took Martin Delaney seriously as he read the Bible in the light of the black experience and indicated that on the basis of his reading of Scripture he could affirm that God was black. Turner wrote:

We have as much right biblically and otherwise to believe that God is a Negroe, as you buckra or white people have to believe that God is a fine looking, symmetrical and ornamented white man. For the bulk of you and all the fool Negroes of the country believe that God is white-skinned, blue eyed, straight haired, projected nosed, compressed lipped and finely robed white gentleman, sitting upon a throne somewhere in the heavens. Every race of people since time began who have attempted to describe their God by words, or by paintings, or by carvings, or any other form or figure, have conveyed the idea that the God who made them and shaped their destinies was symbolized in themselves, and why should not the Negroe believe that he resembles God as much as other people? . . . we certainly protest against God being white at all.[2]

When contemporary black theology is read in this light, the symbol of blackness used by black theologians to relate God to the plight of oppression in North America is seen to be one of the givens of the black community, not a concept created in 1960 or thereabouts. Something of a rough outline for black theology was already present in the black community. As black people searched the Scriptures for themselves, a conversation between the biblical content and the contemporary context ensued. In this contact between the biblical text and the experience of oppression, they began to draw the conclusion that God meant them for freedom and that God was identified with them in their struggle for meaning and freedom. This led Marcus Garvey, a prophet of black liberation, to claim that black people, like the children of Israel, were captives in the white man's land and it was God's will that black people be set free. Garvey devoted his life to the explication of black pride and black dignity as the foundation of black community.

There was certainly no need for Bishop Turner or Marcus Garvey to exegete Scripture or the world that oppressed them in the light of a white ideal. For them the blackness of God ensured the sanctity and humanity of the black community. Hence Garvey could say: "We negroes believe in the God of Ethiopia, the everlasting God—God the Father, God the Son, and God the Holy Ghost, the one God of all ages. This is the God in whom we believe, but we shall worship him through the spectacles of Ethiopia."[3] Black people read the Bible in a way that informed them that God's freedom challenged all forms of bondage in the world. Black people's reading of Scripture made it very clear that the God who made the world wills the freedom of all people. Although they lived in a world in which human bondage threatened the power of freedom, the gospel for them was that God's freedom breaks the power of bondage and offers to the victims of oppression the possibility to be free.

BLACK THEOLOGY AND THE CIVIL RIGHTS MOVEMENT

The role of the black church in the development of black theology reached a high point in two significant movements that emerged in the 1950s and 1960s in North America: the civil rights movement led by the Baptist preacher Martin Luther King, Jr., and the black power movement led by Stokely Carmichael and Malcolm X, the latter the son of a Baptist preacher. The black power movement is related to the black church not only because the term "black power" was coined by a Baptist preacher from Harlem, Adam Clayton Powell, Jr., at a rally in Chicago in May 1965, but also because its philosophy of black dignity and black determination had its roots in the teaching of black church leaders such as Nat Turner, Denmark Vesey, Bishop Henry Turner, and Marcus Garvey.

These two movements went in different directions in that the civil rights movement aimed at a reformation of American life and the black power movement demanded a changing of the structures of oppression. But each in significant ways had immense influence on the development and articulation of black theology.

In the midst of the black power struggle, which came to a head with the issuing of the Black Manifesto by James Forman to the white religious establishment, a little-known theologian published his first book, *Black Theology and Black Power*, in which he contended that black power was the power of Jesus Christ. "The existence of the Church is grounded exclusively in Christ. And in twentieth-century America, *Christ means Black Power!*" declared James Cone.[4] In a chapter on "Black Church and Black Power," Cone says that his understanding of black power was not strange to the black church but, rather, emerged from its life and teaching. While grounding his work in the black power movement, and at the same time calling into question the love ethic of the civil rights movement, Cone said, "Some Black preachers, like the Rev. Highland Garnet, even urged outright rebellion against the evils of white power. He knew that appeals to 'love' or 'good will' would have little effect on minds warped by their own high estimation of themselves and therefore he taught that the spirit of liberty is a gift from God and God thus endows the slave with the zeal to break the chains of slavery."[5] He further points out that the black power movement emerged out of the civil rights movement because black people had become disenchanted with Martin Luther King's emphasis on Jesus' demand to love the enemy.

On the other hand, Major Jones and Deotis Roberts, while using the symbols of blackness and liberation, ground their theologies more in the reformist wing of the civil rights movement. Hence, nonviolence, integration, and reconciliation are viable goals of their theologies. Jones could say that it was not crucial to be a black person; what was important was being a person. "To say that I am a man among men, it would seem, means infinitely more than merely to say that I am a Black man or a white man. To be Black or to be white is merely incidental, but to assert that 'I am a man' is essential."[6] In contrast, Cone regards the denial of blackness as the loss of identity and the basis of sin in the black community. "If we are to understand sin and what it means to Black people, it is necessary to be Black and also a participant in the Black liberation struggle. . . . Sin then for Black people is the loss of identity."[7] The difference in perspective presented in these two approaches to black theology is due not only to Cone's attempt to develop an experiential model for black theology in contrast to the Jones/ Roberts attempt to ferret out a theologico-ethical model that tries to give substance to love's requirements in a situation of racism; it is due also to the different emphases in the civil rights and black power movements to which all these theologians relate. Deotis Roberts dissociates himself from the more militant stance represented by James Cone when he states: "Many Blacks who are not Christians are associated with 'the religion of Black Power.' A Black theologian who operates from the Christian faith has difficulty being heard in this company. . . . A Christian theologian is not an interpreter of the religion of Black Power."[8]

BLACK THEOLOGY AND JUSTIFICATION BY FAITH

Although we referred to the Jones/Roberts explication of black theology as the theologico-ethical model and to Cone's as experiential or, more fittingly, "A Theology of the Black Experience," it is clear that Cone's work has theologico-ethical emphases and the Jones/Roberts model draws on the black experience; more fundamentally, however, the central thrust uniting these two approaches is their emphasis on justification by faith. There is a similarity between Martin Luther's breakthrough in the sixteenth century and that of black Americans in the second half of the twentieth century, but there is also a difference: while Luther's search for a gracious God led him in the discovery of his identity, black people's search for their identity led them to the discovery of a gracious God.

If Paul Althaus is correct in saying that the central questions occupying Luther's thought were *(a)* What does God intend to do with sinful humanity? *(b)* What is God's relationship toward me? and *(c)* How does God feel about me?[9] then it becomes readily apparent that similar concerns fired the imaginations of black theologians as they related God to the search for dignity and peoplehood in the black community. Faith became for black people the way out of Egypt, and the exodus became for them the paradigm of what God was about in the world. The God of the exodus is on the side of the black community leading them out of enslavement under white power toward the promised land of a new humanity. The living God does more than lead his people out of slavery; he comes to destroy the power of the enslaving society. "Christ is the Liberator and the Christian faith promises 'deliverance to the captives.' It promises to let the oppressed go free."[10]

Black theologians take great care to point out that in the light of the exodus motif and the New Testament understanding of Christ as liberator, it is very clear how God feels and what God intends to do with the oppressors and the oppressed.

> . . . he has scattered the proud in the imagination of their hearts, he has put down the mighty from their thrones, and exalted those of low degree. . . . God is at work, to pluck up and break down, to destroy and to overthrow, to build and to plant. For behold a king is born in the city of David, a savior who is Christ the Lord . . . a babe wrapped in swaddling clothes and lying in a manger. Behold, this child is set for the falling and rising of many in Israel . . . [Paul Lehmann, *Ethics in a Christian Context* (New York: Harper and Row, 1976) p. 99].

The cardinal point in the doctrine of justification is the victory of God's love over everything that contradicts and opposes it. Black theology affirms that in Jesus Christ, God entered human history and engaged the forces of oppression in combat and has decisively defeated them. The power of whiteness has been broken as blackness has become the symbol of authentic humanity. In a world in which white skin meant social privilege and advantage and black skin meant inferiority, the Good News is that the freedom of God has broken the power of human bondage and black people can accept their blackness. James Cone echoes Martin Luther when he states: "The Bible, it is important to note, does not consist of units of infallible truth about God or Jesus. Rather, it tells the story of God's will to redeem humankind from sin, death and Satan. According to the New Testament witnesses, God's decisive act against these powers happened in Jesus' life, death and resurrection."[11] "Though the decisive battle against evil has been fought and won, the war, however, is not over."[12]

It is because the battle against white domination and enslavement has been won that the themes of protest and identity formation have become the main key in which black theologians have interpreted the doctrine of justification by faith. Black people protest against a world in which injustice reigns because the Good News is that, in Jesus Christ the liberator, God has defeated the powers of death and the devil. God, in saying yes to the oppressed, has said no to all who would deny them the right to be human. Because the battle against injustice, economic exploitation, and racism has been won, the present situation in which death reigns must be regarded as temporary.

As hope is grounded in God's decisive work in the life, death, and resurrection of Jesus Christ, black people must believe that change is already taking place in the present situation. And this is what faith must mean in the context of oppression: that the present order of injustice is passing. Because of God's gracious action in Jesus Christ toward the oppressed, faith means freedom from the false estimate of the self as inferior to other selves. What God has effected historically in the life, death, and resurrection of Jesus Christ, he accomplishes daily through the justification of people who have claimed their freedom as sons and daughters of God and who say no to all that would encroach on their freedom. Therefore, liberation becomes the content of justification. In a world in which the white church often calls people to its ways rather than God's ways, black theology becomes the people's voice of protest against white supremacy and the attempt of white people to play God in the area of race relations. In this regard liberation is shouting that exploitation and victimization resulting from racism do not have their foundation in God's will but in the attempt of oppressors to pretend they are God. Hence black theologians, whether they sought to develop a theology of the black experience or a theologico-ethical statement aimed at exposing the contradictions between the American way of life and the gospel of liberation, could voice their protest against the sin of idolatry implicit in the practice of racism. Therefore racism was exposed not only for its sin against self, but against God.

Black theology's exposure of the sin of racism pointed it up for what it is: the very basis of sin in that it constitutes the attempt of people to deceive themselves by pretending they are God. In protest against this idolatrous use of skin color, black theologians reversed categories and referred to whiteness as evil and blackness as the point of departure for talk about authentic humanity. One of the values of this form of protest is that it forces white people to rethink the meaning of whiteness. In the cruel world of oppression, whiteness has always symbolized exploitation and dehumanization for black people. Its aim has often been the domestication of black people. But because the battle has been won against the tyrants of racism, injustice, and evil, "Black people know that white people do not have the last word on Black existence." This realization forced black theologians not only to focus on protest as a consequence of their being justified by faith, but to begin with some intentionality to formulate an understanding of identity formation in the black community.

Just as protest is a form of affirmation, since it has its basis in God's action in justification, so affirmation is also the hidden side of protest. Only in recent years, however, have black theologians allowed the needs of the black community to determine the theological agenda. Not until James Cone's third book, *The Spirituals and the Blues* (1972), did we see a sustained attempt by the leading black theologian to allow the agenda of the black community to determine the shape and content of black theology. Prior to this, Cone used Karl Barth, Paul Tillich, and Jean-Paul Sartre to help him protest against the atrocities of white racism. This shift of emphasis gave black theology an opportunity to deal with the empowerment of the black community.

While black theology should not lose sight of the divine no addressed to the perpetrators of oppression, it should begin to give equal time to the divine yes addressed to the victims of oppression. Indeed, this is to suggest that justification must look toward sanctification. Response in obedience to the divine Word is the crucial element here. This would force the black community to deal with the dynamics of its community and to ask awkward questions about classism and sexism and the black communities' relationship to oppression in Third World nations. To ask about the divine presence in the community of the oppressed would lead us to ask whether or not those who benefit from the American way of life participate in the exploitation of Third World nations.

BLACK THEOLOGY AND SANCTIFICATION

In an attempt to get further insight into the empowerment of the black community, we ask if justification by faith is enough. Does faith need something more? In *God of the Oppressed*, James Cone has intimated that a significant role for black theology has to do with the analysis of the structures of oppression; hence, the *more* that faith needs is a social theory that will give clues to procedures and methods for dealing with the demonic structures of oppression. It seems clear that, for James Cone, the *more* that justification by faith needs is Marxism. This insight is significant if black theology is to take Latin American theology seriously.

And yet, the warning of a Baptist preacher is to be taken seriously. Dr. J. H. Jackson, president of the National Baptist Convention, which has a membership of over six million people, has pointed out that for black theology to see Marxist theory as an interpretive tool is for black theology to become a theology of polarization. Dr. Jackson suggests that James Cone's use of the symbol "blackness" also leads to polarization, not only between black people and white people, but among black people. Although James Cone's explication of the symbol "blackness" is often misleading, if Dr. Jackson grasped the double meaning it has for Cone, both its ontological and physical meanings, he would begin to understand that the term refers not only to a people whose skin color is black but to all who are in solidarity with the oppressed.

However, the point of Jackson's criticism remains, that whatever symbols or categories black theology uses should not result in its alienation from the black church but should be a way of giving theology back to the church. In referring to Cone's articulation of black theology, Jackson states: "When he arrives at the color of Jesus, Professor Cone does it by the hands of dialectical materialism. But when he speaks of his rich religious experiences that he has encountered in the teaching of his parents and in the great tradition of the historic AME Church, he is then standing on another level of Christian experience and Christian insights."[13] Indeed, Jackson seems to be suggesting that black theology should use symbols derived from the black church. There is no need for black theologians to go to Europe and borrow from Karl Marx. Jackson suggests that the clue may be in the power and the presence of the Holy Spirit: "There is available to all mankind the power and the presence of the Spirit of God that has and will sustain the prisoners who are incarcerated for truth while it brings a spirit of uneasiness as well as a sense of guilt and shame upon the persons who hold the keys which fasten the chains, bind the limbs of the prisoners and lock the doors which hold the innocent sufferers."[14]

Directions for the future of black theology should come from the black church. Justification must ask for sanctification. Black theology must begin to take root in the contemporary black church as it inquires about the divine activity in the world. Its task in conjunction with its articulation of human freedom, which is God's gift to his church through the life, death, and resurrection of Jesus Christ, is to begin to ask about the formulation of the divine presence in the world. Perhaps a part of what this means for the future of black theology is that as sanctification is affirmed as liberation, the theologico-ethical method of Jones and Roberts, and the experiential method of Cone, will be included in a dialogical method in which divine power will become the point of departure for talk about what God is doing in his church and world. This would not mean that the concerns of the black community would be minimized; but if black power could be defined as the search for black humanity and freedom, then black power would be rooted in divine power. As divine power is related to black power, an encounter between the divine content and the contemporary context takes place. Because liberation is the aim of sanctification, black theology must call attention to the personal and social dimensions of sin as well as the personal and social dimensions of sanctification. Very often when the black church talks about the sanctified life, it is referring specifically to sanctification from sins such as fornication, smoking, and the like. What this emphasis does is to focus on the personal. The importance of this emphasis is in its pointing out that the sin enslaving people is not merely social but inward and personal. It further forces people to deal with the enslavement of the will and the breaking of the inner bondage which binds them. Its weakness is its neglect of the social dimension. A social understanding of sanctification is needed.

A new social understanding of the sanctified life would indicate that action in the name of justice and participation in the changing of unjust structures are part of what it means to be Christian. As divine power is related to black power, the changing of the individual and the changing of the world are not seen as two separate events but as two aspects of the same event. As divine power is disclosed to us, God's will for our lives is made known and we begin to understand that something is wrong with our world. We discover in the manifestation of divine power in our community that something is wrong with the way our world is structured. In the light of the divine activity in our midst, we discern that the social and economic order fails to meet human needs. It becomes clear that we have produced systems of production to enrich a few and impoverish others. As we discern divine power at work in the world, we note that the human family is divided into oppressors and oppressed. We learn that social sin is entrenched in the very fabric of the social and economic order.

As the victims of oppression respond and participate in the divine presence, they are transformed as they begin to turn the world upside down (cf. Acts 17:6). In the exodus of the children of Israel and in the life, death, and resurrection of Jesus of Nazareth, oppressed people understand clearly that the divine presence is associated with justice for the poor and that divine power is at work in the world overthrowing unjust structures. Hence, as the divine content is related to the contemporary context, black power becomes more than a calling into question of unjust structures. As black power is grounded in divine power, the oppressed become participants in the creation of a new order. The vision that impels them is of the sanctified community—a community in which people are respected not because of their achievements and accomplishments but because of their presence.

No more shall there be in it
an infant that lives but a few days,

or an old man who does not fill out his days,
for the child shall die a hundred years old,
and the sinner a hundred years old shall be accursed.
They shall build houses and inhabit them;
they shall plant vineyards and eat their fruit.
They shall not build and another inhabit;
they shall not plant and another eat;
for like the days of a tree shall the days of my people be,
and my chosen shall enjoy the work of their hands

(Isa. 65:20–22, RSV).

NOTES

1. Martin Delaney, cited by Gayraud Wilmore, *Black Religion and Black Radicalism* (Garden City, N.Y.: Doubleday, 1972), p. 153.

2. Henry Turner, cited by Gayraud Wilmore, *Black Religion and Black Radicalism*, p. 173.

3. Amy Jacques-Garvey, ed., *Philosophy and Opinions of Marcus Garvey* (New York: Atheneum, 1974), p. 44.

4. James H. Cone, *Black Theology and Black Power* (New York: Seabury, 1969), p. 112.

5. Ibid., p. 96.

6. Major J. Jones, *Black Awareness* (Nashville: Abingdon, 1971), p. 68.

7. James H. Cone, *A Black Theology of Liberation* (Philadelphia: J. B. Lippincott, 1970), p. 196.

8. J. Deotis Roberts, *Liberation and Reconciliation* (Philadelphia: Westminster Press, 1971), p. 21.

9. See Paul Althaus, *Theology of Martin Luther* (Philadelphia: Fortress Press, 1966), p. 181.

10. Roberts, *Liberation and Reconciliation*, p. 32.

11. James H. Cone, *God of the Oppressed* (New York: Seabury, 1975), p. 110.

12. James H. Cone, *Black Theology and Black Power*, p. 40.

13. J. H. Jackson, *Nairobi: A Joke, a Junket, or a Journey* (Nashville: Townsend Press, 1976), p. 75.

14. Ibid., p. 77.

6

God and the Black Religious Experience

This chapter seeks to look critically and carefully at two religious expressions of the Caribbean that could not be adequately covered in the earlier account of the church and black people in the Caribbean. They are Revivalism and Rastafarianism, two extremes on the continuum of the struggle for black identity in the Caribbean. Although their emphases are different, both are responses to black oppression in the Caribbean, and both developed new and vital dimensions for the black religious experience there. A consideration of Rastafarianism will include attention to the contribution of Marcus Garvey , because the Garvey movement provided the theological and philosophical substance of Rastafarianism.

The Caribbean Council of Churches (see pp. 84–85) did not speak for the Rastafarians or the Revivalists, because each group rejected the European model that was to some extent reflected in the church. For theology to ignore these two groups is to fail to take the black religious experience seriously as the point of departure for talk about God and humanity. The church that would be a redemptive force in the Caribbean must listen to what these two groups are saying, and then be willing to dialogue with them, if it wants to be relevant.

The mainline churches have adopted an air of respectability, which is to say that emotion is suppressed, motion and rhythm are lacking, worship is formalized, persons living in common-law relationships are not welcome, the poor feel conspicuous in their old clothing—all of which has meant that the masses are not at home in mainline church worship. To express themselves naturally in religion, these people have turned to the cults, especially Revivalism, whose goal is redemption, and Rastafarianism, which seeks black solidarity and black dignity.

REVIVALISM

Bedwardism

Revivalism, also known as Pocomania in the Caribbean, is a modern expression of West African myalism (see chap. 2), offering redemption to its adherents. The traditional exclusiveness associated with the church as an institution turned the masses of black Jamaicans to Revivalism.

Alexander Bedward, the father of Revivalism, gave to the people a hope that in him a deliverer had emerged for blacks. Addressed at first as "Shepherd" by his followers, Bedward changed his title to "Incarnation of Jesus Christ" in 1920, with the promise that he would ascend to heaven on December 31, 1920, thereby destroying the rule of white people and establishing the kingdom of Bedwardism on earth. "I myself am Jesus Christ; I was crucified," said Bedward, and the people looked to him as Messiah and called him "Lord." Thousands sold their lands and houses and traveled to Kingston, perhaps with the expectation of accompanying Bedward to heaven.[1] The people began to talk about another Christmas day, "and of another prophet who was to the wise foolishness but whom the common people heard gladly."[2] *The Daily Gleaner* (Kingston) commented:

> Yesterday there was great excitement at the railway. Every train brought in a large number of people, men, women and children all bound for August Town. But they came from Colon as well on a steamer traveling across seas to see their "Lord of August Town" ascend. In King Street all tram cars traveling to Hope Gardens were besieged by men, women and children, some infants in arms, others hardly able to help themselves but they were all bundling in with their clothes, baskets and fowls. All have sold out to come up and see the Lord and master. . . .[3]

Finding himself unable to ascend to heaven, Bedward had to postpone the event, yet this did not destroy the people's faith in him. Perhaps the real genius of Bedward was that he attempted to make a connection between black religion and Christianity. Out of his movement grew the later Revivalist cults.

Revivalist Doctrine and Practice

What is the role of Revivalism in helping black people in the Caribbean to be more fully human? Does it serve as a context in which the identity problem caused by slavery can be meaningfully addressed? Is the hope that the Revivalists offer able to liberate the victims of oppression? Revivalism certainly offers a context in which people can express themselves in their own way, and perhaps above all it provides a setting in which black people can accept themselves, affirming that they are accepted by their God in history. Mammy Welliston, a noted woman Revivalist in the 1920s, once said: ''I didn't know to pray until I got the spirit, and the spirit teaches me to pray and sends me on the highways and the hedges to bid others to come and tell what a sweet savior I found. Jesus is Savior in need and Savior indeed. There is not a friend like the loving Savior.''[4]

The Revivalists, as Mammy Welliston's words suggest, sought to incorporate Christian terms and took the name of Jesus Christ quite seriously. Even at this point, however, Jesus seems to have been one spirit among others. The incorporation of African and ''Christian'' symbols in worship appears to be one way in which Revivalists deal with their identity tensions. They are not able to embrace Chrisitianity as the mainline churches portray it, because that does not take sufficient cognizance of the African background, but they can accept adaptations of it which appeal to their experience. Revivalism's reliance on myalism and African symbols in worship indicates its inability to abandon black religion. This willingness to bring both the African and the European worlds together is the significant contribution of Revivalism. The Revivalists' interpretation of black religion is the point of departure for spanning the distance between the two worlds. The practical ways in which the Revivalists were able to deal with two worlds, one black and the other white, and thereby create space to live creatively, are found in (*a*) the context of their worship and (*b*) the content of their worship.

The worship place of the Revivalists is often designated by a sign or symbol indicating the name of the meeting place. ''Coming into the yard, the first object seen is a 'pole' or 'seal' (sometimes called the center). This may be only a tall pole with a flag attached to it which bears the name of the Church or some mystical symbols, or it may be a pole with a boxlike miniature house (ark) at the top. . . . Often a Bible or other sacred object is placed in the box, or it may be said that the house is the office of the spirit.''[5] Most of the meeting places have dirt floors, a table, and pictures of Jesus Christ hanging on the walls. The most important book is the Bible, and it is not infrequent to find two or more Bibles on the table. ''Many leaders possess, or have access to, one or more of the books of magic published by the de Laurence Company of Chicago. These books are forbidden by law in Jamaica, but many are secreted in the island. The sixth and seventh Book of Moses is the favorite title.''[6]

Inside the meeting place there is usually a large wooden cross, which is carried in procession at baptismal services. In addition there are numerous banners and placards. Often a red flag is among the banners. It is used in a ceremony to ''cut down'' evil spirits.

Jars of water, called ''consecrated,'' are always found at Revivalist meeting places. A ''mother'' may have attached to her belt a pair of scissors, which symbolically may be used to ''cut clean'' evil spirits at the beginning of a service. Also hanging from the mother's belt may be a whistle and a key. The whistle may be used to warn the spirits that the service is about to begin, or it may be used to stop the singing or to calm a person who is spirit-possessed. The key belongs to the spirit.*

The drum is the most important musical instrument used by the Revivalist. "Usually a period of preliminary drumming precedes the appearance of the leader and the beginning of the main part of the service. . . . Prayers by the leader, prayers given individually, but simultaneously and aloud by the members, Bible reading, announcements, singing, preaching, 'laboring in the spirit,' spirit possession, and public testimonials alternate the brief intervals."[7] Favorite hymns are, "How Sweet the Name of Jesus Sounds," "I Heard the Voice of Jesus Say," and "Sun, Moon and Stars—They Shine So Bright."

The tension between black religion and Chrisitianity, and how it may be dealt with, is suggested by this extract from a Revivalist's sermon:

> Did you ever see a white preacher west of Slipe Pen Road? [Chorus: "No!"] If it wasn't for these small missions bringing the gospel of Jesus Christ to the poor people there would be more people in prison than there are now. [Another leader asked: "Is Zionism superstitious voodoo?"] I say it is the spirit of the Lord Jesus Christ. Oh, yes! We haven't been to no college. We have learned from the spirit. Some people can't get the spirit because they are not clean. They are not pure; they have not lived the right way. Some people don't believe that we can heal by the spirit, but we are going to have testimonials later tonight and we are going to have faith healing. Sometimes there are bystanders on the outside who do not believe that the spirit can heal, but when they see what we can do, they become believers.[8]

The baptismal service in the Revivalist cults is another instance where both worlds meet. The Revivalists demand baptism by immersion. John 3:1–15 is usually cited to show that a person must be born again in order to enter heaven, and this usually means, for the Revivalist, immersion. One is not required to lead a devout life before baptism, nor to attend instructions at the meeting place. Preparation of the candidate is the work of the spirit only.

I should like here to draw on my own experience and recollections. The Revivalist spirit had spilled over into the Baptist Church in which I was brought up as a boy in St. Thomas, Jamaica. Although it was a mainline church, its celebration of the sacraments exemplified the influence of Revivalism. I recall how my baptismal experience at the age of twelve brought together the African world and the Christian world. It was early Good Friday morning, about 2:00 A.M. All the candidates for baptism

* This was a common experience in my childhood. N.L.E.

met in the church with the "mothers" and the deacons, and being moved by the spirit we sang and testified. After much prayer in the spirit we all set out, with the church mothers and deacons leading, and all of us dressed in white, to the place where our sins would be washed away. It was about three miles that we walked in the early morning, many of us children not quite understanding the ways of the spirit. My father was the minister and, being filled with the Revivalist spirit, he asked each of us if we believed in Jesus Christ. Being assured that we did, he then immersed us in the river. Standing close to him with towels in hand to cover us and ready to calm us if we were overpowered by the spirit was "the water mother," who took charge of each of us and safely guided us out of the river.

My first Communion service after baptism was similar to the one described below, held after baptism in a Revivalist meeting in October 1953. The main differences between the Communion service after my baptism and the one described here were the fact that my father had had theological training, and in our church we had an organ instead of drums.

The meeting began with the usual handclapping, drumming, singing, praying and Bible reading. Excerpts from the installment preaching on this occasion are: "I know you must be happy finding yourselves in the wonderful kingdom of Jesus Christ. . . . I want you to believe tonight that Jesus Christ saves, that He sanctifies, that He heals . . . your sins. All of you who are here tonight who believe in Jesus Christ, repent and be baptized for the remission of your sins. . . . Love the Lord with all your soul and with all your heart. . . . I am thanking the Lord tonight that there are no fights, no quarrels, no contentions, no murders, but just a happy set of people. Am I right? Amen. . . . Now, brothers and sisters, I feel wonderful in my heart tonight. . . . I am for the Church of God in Christ. What is the Church of God in Christ? I am not telling you that I am Jesus Christ. I know I am a sinner saved by grace, saved by Jesus Christ. . . . [9]

These were some of the manifestations of being "in the spirit." During the Communion service there were many believers who were "in the spirit."

Many black people, as they climbed the social ladder, tended to leave the Revivalists and seek affiliation with the Baptists. The black middle class in the Caribbean still hold membership in the Baptist, Methodist, and other mainline denominations. But since educational achievement and economic status, homeownership, and a stable two-parent family are among the requirements for middle-class status in the Caribbean, the masses of people still seek an answer to their quest for meaning in the context of the Revivalist sects. The black middle-class person who qualifies can become a member of the mainline church; however, a large percentage of the Caribbean does not qualify for membership in these churches. The mainline churches in the Caribbean are not yet able to cope effectively with the problem of illegitimate births and concubinage. The head matron of Kingston Jubilee Maternity Hospital pointed out that of the number of patients the hospital had in one year, 801 were married, 2,191 were unmarried. During that year, there were 642 legitimate births and 1,849 illegitimate births. Both the unmarried mothers and the illegitimate children would not have been received in my father's church or in any of the middle-class churches in Jamaica.

In *The Church in the New Jamaica,* J. Merle Davis points out that:

> The problem is economic as well as spiritual. In talking with such a couple [unmarried], the man said: "We have long wished to change this life, but we are not able to do so. I need a pair of shoes and suit of clothing in which to get married and cannot afford them." I have seen men who wanted to get married trying for fifteen years to get together enough money to clothe themselves and their families for a wedding. Such parents may be living in a cane trash hut along with ten children—all sleeping on the damp earth. What can the church do to help such people . . . ?"[10]

It is at this level that the Revivalist cults are able to provide a context for black people to begin to understand themselves in the light of their quest for freedom in history. The babies, whether legitimate or illegitimate, are blessed in the meeting places; mothers and fathers irrespective of their marital status are accepted in the meeting places, thus assuring both children and parents that they are accepted by their God. My father's church and the Jamaica Council of Churches could not accept the people as they were; black people first had to become middle class, and then they could become members. The Revivalist cults sought to teach the middle-class churches that there is no need to suppress the black religious experience, the black religious identity. This religious context that the Revivalists provide for black people made them aware that they could "enjoy church," that worship and praise of God were to be enjoyed rather than experienced as a duty. As the Revivalist wove together tenets of Christianity with black religion, black people found an identity of their own; they could pray long prayers, sing their gospel songs, engage in loud preaching and emotional responses, and spend all day in church. It was this opportunity for black people to identify themselves that made worshiping God at the meeting place an extension of the family gathering.

The Revivalists in the Caribbean taught us that black people do not have to leave their black culture behind as they seek to worship their God, because "religion is the substance of culture and culture is the form of religion."[11] And since the Caribbean church as a middle-class institution is an expression of middle-class values, it does not speak with specificity to the innermost needs of the masses of Caribbean people.

An unfortunate assumption of the poor and the weak is that they have nothing to offer. Sometimes the victims of society see themselves as empty vessels to be filled. This is illustrated in the prayer of a black man in Spanish Town.

O Lord, me heart is full, but me is poo ting, not able to find word to tell de my want and desire. Me know not how to pray, nor what to pray for, but me heart is open to de like a well widout cover, and me come dis night, hungring and thirsting, to eat de bread of life, and bring me empty pitcher, like de woman of Samaria, to draw water out of de well of Salvation. O send me not empty away. Bless me, even me also, O our Fader, for dow hast promis if poo sinner call pon de, dow will hear dem, for dy ear dont heavy dat it cannot hear, neider dy arm shorten dat dow cannot save.[12]

From what we have seen of the context and content of worship, we know that black people did not come to their worship empty, certainly not at a revival meeting. They brought their African ethos with them, and this provided the context in which to carry out their search for identity. Black people brought with them their world of the spirit and their belief in dreams, and their confidence that the Spirit of God would effect healing at the Revivalist meeting. This was the religious context in which their search for theological significance occurred. Dreams and the belief in the power of the spirits played an important role in the black religious experience in Jamaica, as illustrated by one Alexander who was told "in the spirit" when someone would die, and also was informed in a dream what medicine to use for healing.

It is exactly forty-one years since I was converted. I was called by the spirit of God. As I was called, I was down on my back on one place in the room eleven months. I couldn't come out at all, only lying in one place, the spirit taken away from me and I learning the mystery of God. Then one day I got Psalms One Hundred Sixteen. . . . And after I lay down, in the night, I was taken away in the spirit to Browns Town. I din't walk 'pon the earth; I flew in the air to Browns Town, I saw the master. And he had a little book, and he spread it upon the earth, and I couldn't see. And he read out of it, "Parson Clark, your time is up on earth." And I saw a beautiful vessel waiting for him. . . . And he said to me, "It is finished with Parson Clark." And the foundation of Browns Town groaned.[13]

In that same dream, Jesus gave Alexander authority to become the leader of the congregation. "And he said, 'now take charge of these sheep and mind them for me.' . . . And I said, 'some of these sheep are very trespass.' And he said, 'you desire these trespass sheep with cords, and the cords are the word of God.' "[14]

Alexander did not allow the world around him to define him. For him to have allowed the world to define him, he would have had to relinquish the power to identify himself. In his dream the Spirit of God called him apart for a special task, which gave meaning to his identity. He was to find his identity in his community. Perhaps Alexander makes the connection for us between God and the black religious experience. It is the relationship between blackness and faith, it is learning that God's call to identify oneself is inseparable from the community to which one belongs. In Alexander's dream, Jesus said to him, " 'You desire to bind these trespass sheep with cords, and the cords are the word of God.' And [Alexander] said, 'Sir, when it becomes dark, how shall I see to mind those sheep from the lion and the wolf—from the Devil and Satan?' And he burst out with a great light which passed to the four corners of the world.' '¹⁵ God's call to black humanity, according to Alexander, is inseparable from the revelatory character of the black community. In the context of this community, black people pursue their vocation to be free.

It must be borne in mind that the majority of black people who are adherents of the Revivalist cults live in dreary, one-room dwellings. Unemployment is high. Those who do work, both men and women, are in low-paid, unskilled or semiskilled jobs. The unemployed do almost anything to stay alive. The hope for salvation is particularly strong in this context. The challenge for these black people is to affirm their humanity and be human at the same time, and Revivalism has provided the means for them to meet the challenge. What is their understanding of Revivalism?

Revivalists believe that the world is peopled with spirits. Michael and Gabriel are the two most revered and loved spirits. After Michael and Gabriel are "Samuel, Raphael, Jeremiah, Jesus Christ, God, Miriam, Mary, Satan, Holy Ghost, Moses, Ezekiel, Uriel, Casuel, Solomon, David, Joshua, Isaiah, Daniel, Rutibel, Matthew, Mark, Luke, John, Peter, James, Ariel, Shadrach, Meshach, Abednego, Caleb, Nathaniel, Tharsis, Seraph, Melshezdek, Constantine and the Royal Angel.''¹⁶ This is certainly not an exhaustive list of the Jamaican spirits, most of whom are from the Old and New Testaments. The main task of the spirits is to protect the initiate from danger. To be a member of the Revivalist cult is to have the good spirits as one's guardian.

In addition to the heavenly spirits, there are the spirits of dead relatives who can either hurt or help the living. The dead through their spirits are able to protect their relatives from evil magic. In order to obtain needed assistance from the spirit of the dead, the relative must be able to concentrate on that particular relative. That of course assumes that one had given the departed an adequate funeral. Failure to be generous to the dead will result in punishment of the bereft family by the spirit of the departed. The spirit of the departed will also punish those who do not "live right.''¹⁷

Rutibel, Satan's assistant, is an evil spirit that haunts all people who have surrendered to Satan's kingdom. Those who are committed to Satan's kingdom wither and die.

The main task of the Revivalist is to enlist the help of the spirits through private or public ritual, so that the congregation may be blessed by the spirits and hence avoid their wrath. The ordinary believer is able, through visions and dreams, to communicate with the spirits, especially those who may have possessed the believer at some time. Knowing the powers and interests of the various spirits is helpful in determining which spirit to call on for a specific situation. The following list is helpful in showing how they are understood in the Revivalist cults:

Christ is merciful.
Gabriel is the head angel around the throne of Almighty God, Minister of the Midnight wind; cross and warlike.
Jeremiah is the chief prophet because ''him suffer deep.'' He cuts and clears away ''destruction.''
Isaiah says that men must fast and pray deep to get the teaching from the holy prophets.
God sends death and judgment messages.
Michael is the minister of the Lord's Day (also called the Angel of Peace).
Samuel is the minister of Blood.
Rutibel concentrates on evil deeds.
Raphael is chief minister of the Archangel group; minister of the General Wind.
Matthew, Mark, Luke and John can be helpful to everyone.
Satan may be used if an important case is in court.
Solomon was black.
Moses was able to pass many miracles.
Casuel was guardian of the heathen at the time of Adam and Eve.
Shadrach, Meshack and Abednego were baptized in a Furnace of Fire. . . .
God and the saints are for everybody.[18]

The main function of Revivalism is certainly not to explain God, but to help clarify the meaning of black existence, given the mystery of identity in a world peopled by many spirits. In a world in which human existence raises the question concerning the meaning of identity, the Revivalist seems to rely on the help of the spirit in addressing the problem. The problem of identity is answered not merely in relation to the world, but in relation to the spirit. The ideal life is life in the spirit. The goal of the Revivalist meeting is that all present may be possessed by the spirit. When the spirit descends upon one, one cannot resist.

A practical consequence of living in the spirit is that one does not sin. The main sins against which Revivalism counsels are stealing, lying, hatred, criticism, thinking evil, deceitfulness, fornication, being unjust, coveting a neighbor's goods, and placing an evil spirit or spell on a person. Other sins include cruelty to human beings, starving oneself when one has money, taking away a person's freedom, and destroying another person's garden.[19]

The Revivalists are unique not only in their interpretation of life in the spirit, but also in their understanding of fornication. One Revivalist leader illustrates the general attitude to fornication. "We know that people have to get to know each other before they marry. There is no definite trial period; they carry through marriage when they find money. If a man or woman goes from one to another, he is a professional fornicator." Another leader said, "I tell young people to take one person and make yourself comfortable. When you find perfection, that is, one who is satisfactory, marry if you can afford it or live holy with that one person. Don't take two or more at one time."[20]

In marriage we see an attempt to deal with both the European and the African worlds. Polygamy is rejected, and monogamy is advocated, but it is reinterpreted, because marriage as a legal contract is the exception rather than the rule. As couples were admonished by the Revivalist cults to "live holy," the traditional understanding of fornication was rejected. This emphasis made room for a very large percentage of Caribbean peoples who would not otherwise find acceptance in the church.

Revivalism in the Caribbean, apart from providing a context in which black people can identify themselves, also deals with their religious beliefs. This is an important function. These beliefs may seem strange because they are different and, admittedly, are the "cultural fragments" of primitive people, but they are a vital part of the world of the Caribbean. To treat them as inconsequential is to fail these people theologically. The Revivalist cults must lead the Christian church, and any theology that would speak with cogency to the Caribbean, to use the symbols of black religious experience as expressive tools in structuring a religion that would have redemptive power for this community. Theology in the Caribbean must arise from the black religious experience if it seeks the redemption of these people.

THE RASTAFARIANS

The Garvey Movement

The story of black humanity in the Caribbean is unfinished without a review of the contribution of the Rastafarians. The Rastafarian cults become important in the context of this study because they insist that the black religious experience is the only adequate basis for talk about the search for freedom. They differ from the Revivalists in that redemption, for them, is inextricably linked to Ethiopia and its former emperor, Haile Selassie I. Haile Selassie, who was for them the black Christ, became the point of departure for their talk about black humanity in the Caribbean.

In order to understand the contribution of the Rastafarian cult, it is imperative to give theological attention to Marcus Mosiah Garvey, who laid the theological and philosophical basis of Rastafarian thought.

Garvey, the founder of the back-to-Africa movement, became a prophet of black liberation in the Caribbean. He envisioned the return of black people to their homeland. Black people, like the children of Israel, were captives in the white man's land, and it was God's will that they be set free. Garvey wrote:

> As children of captivity we look forward to a new, yet ever old, land of our fathers, the land of God's crowning glory. We shall gather together our children, our treasures and our loved ones, and, as the children of Israel, by the command of God, face the promised land, so in time we shall also stretch forth our hands and bless our country.[21]

Born in Jamaica in 1887, Marcus Garvey belonged to both the nineteenth and the twentieth centuries. He lived in a transitional time and was able to lay out the theological assumptions for black people's understanding of God. In referring to God's relationship to humanity, Garvey wrote:

> When God breathed into the nostrils of man the breath of life, made him a living soul, and bestowed upon him the authority of "Lord of Creation," He never intended that an individual should descend to the level of a peon, a serf, or a slave, but that he should be always man in the fullest possession of his senses and with the truest knowledge of himself. But how changed has man become since creation? We find him today divided into different classes—the helpless imbecile, the dependent slave, the servant and master. These different classes God never created. He created man.[22]

Garvey continued to give substance to his understanding of people's responsibility before God. Humanity, he says, has fallen away from God's plan. There is a distance between people as they are and the way they should be. God meant a person to be "real person." But it is a fact that many black people have deviated from God's ideal for humanity. This is one reason why the black race has stagnated and is "at the foot of the great human ladder." God gave humanity responsibility in the world and over the world; and as the black race affirms the fatherhood of God and the brotherhood of human beings, black people should take control of their world, because this control was given to them by God.[23]

Although Garvey called upon black people to take responsibility for their plight, he was not unaware of the problem of color as it existed in the Caribbean. As a child he grew up with other children in his neighborhood, giving no particular attention to their color. But at fourteen years of age he was jolted when the white minister's daughter, a friend of his, left for school in England and was told by her parents not to write to him because he was a "nigger." It was something Garvey never forgot. And it opened his eyes to the racial discrimination prevalent in Jamaican society. Opportunities for desirable employment, such as training for government jobs, went to white youths. Black boys became the laborers, with an occasional teaching post for an especially bright black person.

Garvey's doctrine of creation included profound insights about how black people should be regarded along with other people in the presence of God. Garvey affirmed that God created all people equal, and to deny this was to insult God Almighty.[24] Implicit in Garvey's doctrine of God as creator was his understanding of anthropology. According to him, the almightiness of God is the foundation for the courage of black people. Black people, who are also appointed by God as "lord of creation," have unlimited power bestowed upon them in their gift of humanity. God has created space for all peoples, and as black people look for their redemption, they must claim the continent God gave them.

> If Europe is for the white man, if Asia is for brown and yellow men, then surely Africa is for the black man. The great white man has fought for the preservation of Europe, the great yellow and brown races are fighting for the preservation of Asia, and four hundred million negroes shall shed, if needs be, the last drop of blood for the redemption of Africa and the emancipation of the race everywhere.[25]

Here Garvey gave a world perspective to black people's talk about God and humanity. Garvey linked the doctrine of creation with black people's search for freedom. In creating black people free, God created them for freedom, declared Garvey. And freedom must continue to be the vision of humanity. In creating black people free, God gave them a place in the world, and God must not be blamed for the bondage of the black race. "God almighty created us all free."[26]

Here Garvey broached the important question concerning the relationship between divine freedom and human responsibility. Although freedom is God's gift to black people, this freedom must be actualized, Garvey believed. "To think that we [black people] were created only to be what we are," said Garvey, "and not what we can make ourselves . . ." is an error. The man who is a real man "is the man who will never give up, the man who will never depend on others to do for him what he ought to do for himself: the man who will never blame God . . . for his condition."[27]

Garvey sought to embody his teaching in his life. Being aware of the predicament of black people, he gave himself unreservedly for their liberation. As a child, he would listen to the most gifted orators, and himself became so gifted as an elocutionist that he was the first teacher of elocution in Jamaica. The freedom of faith, which he calls attention to in the doctrine of creation, had consequences for political freedom. When twenty-seven years old, Garvey organized in Kingston, Jamaica, the Universal Negro Improvement Association and African Communities League. The purpose of the movement was to unite black people throughout the world for the establishment of their own country and government. It seems as if a Revivalist custom had spilled over into Garvey's world as he recalls how the name of the organization was revealed to him: "At midnight, lying flat on my back, the vision and thought came to me that I should name the organization the Universal Negro Improvement Association and African Communities (Imperial) League. Such a name I thought would embrace the purpose of all black humanity."[28]

Garvey took the doctrine of creation to its logical conclusion, that of positing the equality of humanity. In his vision of the new humanity, he could say: "I saw before me then, as I do now, a new world of black men, not peons, serfs, dogs and slaves, but a nation of sturdy men making their impress upon civilization and causing a new light to dawn upon the human race. . . ."[29]

The black Jamaican middle class had a problem with the consequences stemming from Garvey's doctrine of God. Garvey could affirm blackness as God's gift to black people, since God had created humanity in his own image. But they felt that Garvey had insulted them by including the word "Negro" in the title of his movement. Middle-class black Jamaicans never referred to themselves as "Negroes." Only the poor masses of society were called that. The middle class was not at peace with blackness; hence Garvey's doctrine was mainly received by the poor masses of black people, who formed the great majority of Jamaica's population.

Garvey stopped short of saying "God is black," but all indications point to an understanding of a black God. He insisted that, since the white people saw God as white, black people should see God in the light of Ethiopia. "We negroes believe in the God of Ethiopia, the everlasting God—God the Father, God the Son and God the Holy Ghost, the one God of all ages. This is the God in whom we believe, but we shall worship him through the spectacles of Ethiopia."[30]

Garvey also taught that the suffering and resurrection of Jesus Christ were the guarantee that the black race in its struggle for freedom would experience a new birth because of the triumph of Christ's resurrection. Garvey said: "As Christ by His teaching, His sufferings and His death triumphed over His foes, through the resurrection, so do we hope that out of our sufferings and persecutions of today we will triumph in the resurrection of our new born race."[31] In a sermon delivered on Christmas Day 1921, Garvey stated that Jesus Christ is the redeemer and deliverer of fighting and oppressed humankind. Jesus Christ will reconcile the human race and help black people to forget their differences and proclaim peace. Christ is the bringer of life, the life of love and mercy. His suffering and death was for black people's freedom. "Yet even with the great object of the cross before us, even though he overcame death, the grave and hell to demonstrate to us the new life possible to each and every one of us, we have not yet turned from the path of sin to enter into the glory of his eternal kingdom."[32]

Sin, for Garvey, was the loss of identity by black people. To enter the kingdom of freedom and humanity, which Christ made possible through cross and resurrection, black people must be at peace with blackness. Theology became the theme of anthropology for Garvey's exposition of black humanity. According to him, the doctrine of God's love is the basis on which a proper self-understanding must be built. The love of God as the theme of black identity is illustrated in another sermon by Garvey:

> . . . men and women of my race, do you know that the God we love, the God we adore, the God who sent His Son to this world nearly two thousand years ago never created an inferior man? That God we love, that God we worship and adore has created man in his own image, equal in every respect, wheresoever he may be; let him be white, let him be yellow, let him be red, let him be black, God has created him the equal of his brother. He is such a loving God. He is such a merciful God. . . . The God that you worship is a God that expects you to be the equal of other men. The God that I adore is such a God and he could be no other.[33]

The doctrine of the love of God and the doctrine of creation are brought together in the sermon above, as Garvey shows how, together, they are the foundation for black identity. Black people must affirm that they reflect the greatness of God. Blackness is God's gift to black people, and to reject it as God's creation, and as the sign of God's love for them, is to insult God.[34]

An independent Jamaica gave assent to Garvey's contribution by according him the highest honor possible for a Jamaican, by exalting him to the status of national hero. The religious cult called the Rastafarians was primarily responsible for Jamaica's not forgetting the contribution of Marcus Garvey. The Rastafarians, who pressed for black solidarity and social and economic power, constitute an expression of resistance to black oppression. They provide an answer to the problem of black identity in the Caribbean: in regarding the black Messiah as the hope for black liberation.

Bearers of the Messianic Hope: The Rastafarians

The Rastafarians are unique to Jamaica. They constitute a religious cult which believes that Ras Tafari, crowned as Haile Selassie I, Emperor of Ethiopia, King of Kings and Lord of Lords, Conquering Lion of the Tribe of Judah, is God. He himself claimed to be descended from David, through Solomon and the Queen of Sheba, in unbroken line. This messianic cult had its origins in the depression years of the 1930s. Jamaica was governed by a few people who had no feeling for the hungry. The day's wage for black people was twenty-five cents for men and fourteen cents for women. A few Englishmen had the final word on the political and economic destiny of the island. The people who invested in Jamaica did so only for financial gain and not because of any human concern. There was no democratic process involved in the business. The pattern applied in the business world was hierarchical. A handful of white people at the apex of Jamaican society gave the orders and made decisions. There was submission and compliance at the bottom, and there were no tools the victims of society could use to persuade their leaders to act otherwise.

Rastafarianism was born out of the pain of oppression. This pain fired the hope for deliverance. One of the leaders of the cult, Sam Brown, makes a connection between Garvey and the movement. He points out that after Garvey left the scene in 1930, black people were purposeless, and Rastafarianism emerged to give focus and direction to the black masses.[35] The coronation of Haile Selassie in 1930 caused a great stir among black people, and many of them began to study their Bibles more closely. They recalled how Garvey the prophet had said, "Look to Africa where a black king shall arise—this will be the day of your deliverance."[36] The connection with Garvey's prophecy attracted the Garveyites, and this resulted in the incorporation of many of Garvey's ideas into the movement. By 1933 the movement began to teach that Ras Tafari was God, the "King of Kings" and the "Root of David." The main biblical focus for this cult was Revelation, chapters 5 and 19.

> . . . and I saw a strong angel proclaiming with a loud voice, "Who is worthy to open the scroll and break its seals?" And no one in heaven or on earth or under the earth, was able to open the scroll or to look into it, and I wept much that no one was found worthy to open the scroll or to look into it. Then one of the elders said to me, "Weep not; lo, the Lion of the tribe of Judah, the Root of David, has conquered, so that he can open the scroll and its seven seals." . . . On his robe and on his thigh he has a name inscribed, King of kings and Lord of lords (Rev. 5:1–5; 19:16, RSV).

Being steeped in Scripture, the Rastafarians announced the dawn of a new age, which had appeared in the black community with the inauguration of the black king. The Rastafarians regard Jamaica as the Babylon which holds them in captivity. Their existence is marked by suffering and oppression because multiracial Jamaica offers them only captivity in exile. In this state of exile, the Rastafarians, who are the true Israelites, expect the freedom and redemption of black people. They are called to leave Babylon and return to the promised land of Ethiopia, where Haile Selassie fulfilled in the twentieth century the prophecy that a "King would arise out of Jesse's root," as God for all black people and as liberator of the oppressed of the earth.[37]

The twin concepts of the divinity of Haile Selassie and the redemption of black people have distinguished the Rastafarian cult from other movements which seek to create an awareness of black consciousness. One of the positive effects of this call for black redemption and the divinity of a black man is that it has meant a reversal of values for black people. One of the assumptions of many black people, that white is good and black is inferior, was radically called into question through the postulation of a black God. The white-oriented value system that dominated Caribbean society was rejected by the Rastafarians.

During the 1960s a great number of black people in the Caribbean became sympathetic toward the attitudes and ideals of Rastafarianism. This was expressed in large numbers of young people who symbolized their loyalty to the cult by wearing long and unkempt hair, and openly referred to themselves as "black" rather than "Negro."

The Rastafarians complained against the "continuing colonial regime" in Jamaica despite political independence, the cruelty of the police to the victims of poverty, and the absence of justice in the courts of the land. They are identified by their rejection of the "white bias" of Caribbean society, which widens the distance between rich and poor, and the inability of the political leaders to find an answer to the quest for identity of black people. The Rastafarians were also among the first to object to the ownership of key resources in Jamaica by multinational corporations.[38]

In this same period the Rastafarians began to teach that Africa was in Jamaica. This became a call for the Africanization of Jamaica. Black Jamaica did not have to migrate to Africa; there was an inward migration, according to the Rastafarians. In the same way in which one might argue that the kingdom of God is within, so may one claim that Africa is within.[39] At this level the Rastafarians went beyond Garvey, as Garvey had taught that black people should physically return to Africa.

In using their ideology as a response to black oppression, the Rastafarians best represent the emergence of theology as a language arising out of the black religious experience. This is a main plank on which they seek to build black identity.

In referring to the humanity and divinity of God, the Rastafarians insist that talk about God must take on historical moment. God must be experienced within the context of human life. They contend that the divinity of God is revealed in the humanity of the man-God Ras Tafari Selassie I. The Rastafarians point out that to advocate the divinity of Haile Selassie does not make them unchristian. On the contrary, it confirms that they are the only Christians, because Haile Selassie is the reincarnation of Jesus Christ. Jesus Christ had promised to return and has kept his promise in the appearance of the black God.[40]

History, for the Rastafarians, has theological significance. It is the scene of the activity of God. Because of this they pay close attention to the local press for any signs that might indicate the imminent victory of God. The linear concept of history is of first importance. History is not cyclical, it is a journey, a pilgrimage to the promised land.

The Rastafarians bring an existential emphasis to their interpretation of this world. They argue that Christians, in placing an inordinate emphasis on death, do not give enough weight and attention to life now. For the Christian, life on earth is often a prelude to life after death, and a consequence of this tendency is that often the sacredness of history is not regarded with enough seriousness. We are not called to fear death but to celebrate life. The book of Revelation provides the matrix in which the Rastafarian seeks to understand his identity. History is apocalyptic, and there will be a cosmic struggle betweeen justice and oppression. Good shall prevail.

Sin is not merely an individual or personal matter, but also a structural matter. Because of this, Rastafarians attack nations, corporations, empires, and races, applying the teachings of the Ten Commandments to them as well as to individuals.

Prior to the 1960s, the Rastafarian call for black people to reject Jamaica for Ethiopia, where the Christ reincarnate reigned, was not taken seriously. The news media often reported the problems of Ethiopia and presented it as a land certainly not flowing with milk and honey. This made Ethiopia unattractive to many black people. Yet, black Jamaicans have always regarded repatriation as an answer to their social and economic problems, and many of them have gone to West Africa to work. Indeed, migration as an answer to the social ills of one's country has for a long time been a Caribbean way of life. However, the call in recent years by the Rastafarians to Africanize Jamaica seems to offer hope to the majority of black people that Africanization may become a vital spiritual force, as black people seek their God in history.

In calling attention to the man-God Haile Selassie, the Rastafarians have kept alive for the church the place of the God-man Jesus Christ as the bearer of identity. The Rastafarians' man-God has died and they await his reincarnation. The Christian faith witnesses to the resurrection of Jesus Christ as the ground of hope for humanity.

Traditional Christianity seldom depicted God as involved in the blackness of black lives. God was often transcendent without being immanent. The Rastafarians have served to remind the Christian church that the God who would liberate the oppressed from a distorted estimate of themselves cannot be an alien or a foreigner. He cannot be a stranger to blackness. The only concern cannot be the concern of Nicaea: whether or not Jesus is of the same substance as the Father. This must be combined with the identity of Jesus and this becomes the basis of black identity.

NOTES

1. Martha Warren Beckwith, *Black Roadways* (New York: Negro University Press, 1929), p. 168.
2. Ibid., p. 169.
3. Ibid.
4. Ibid., p. 163.
5. *Social and Economic Studies* 5, No. 1 (March 1956): 360.
6. Ibid., p. 362.
7. Ibid., p. 366.
8. Ibid., p. 367.
9. Ibid., p. 371.
10. J. Merle Davis, *The Church in the New Jamaica* (London: International Missionary Council, 1942). p. 36. On a recent visit to the U.S. Virgin Islands, church leaders from the Moravian, Seventh-Day Adventist, Methodist, and Anglican churches called attention to the problems illegitimate births posed for the churches.
11. Paul Tillich, *Theology of Culture* (New York: Oxford University Press, 1959), p. 42.
12. In James M. Phillippo, *Jamaica, Its Past and Present State* (London: Dawson, 1969), pp. 342–43.
13. Beckwith, *Black Roadways*, p. 166.
14. Ibid., p. 167.
15. Ibid.
16. Ibid., p. 344.
17. Ibid.
18. Ibid., p. 345. One of my earliest recollections of a theological discussion is that of my cousin telling me that Jesus is a merciful spirit, but that God is a spirit of wrath. N.L.E.
19. Ibid., p. 347.
20. Ibid.
21. Amy Jacques-Garvey, ed., *Philosophy and Opinions of Marcus Garvey* vol. 1 (New York: Atheneum, 1974), p. 121.
22. Ibid., p. 24.
23. Ibid., pp. 24–25.
24. Ibid., p. 130.
25. Ibid., p. 32.
26. Ibid., p. 37.
27. Ibid., pp. 37–39.
28. In Leonard Barrett, *Soul Force*, (Garden City, N.Y.: Doubleday, 1974), p. 132.
29. Ibid., p. 131.
30. Amy Jacques-Garvey, ed., *Philosophy*, p. 44.
31. Ibid., p. 62.
32. Ibid., p. 84.
33. Ibid., p. 89.
34. Ibid., p. 91.
35. See Barrett, *Soul Force*, p. 158.
36. Ibid.

37. See Rex M. Nettleford, *Identity, Race and Protest in Jamaica* (New York: William Morrow, 1972), pp. 41f.

38. Ibid., p. 46.

39. Ibid., p. 101.

40. See Idris Hamid, ed., *Troubling of the Waters* (San Fernando, Trinidad: Rahaman Printery, 1972), pp. 167–70.

Conclusion:
Toward a Theology of Freedom

The search for freedom in the Caribbean called attention to the inability of colonial theology to address with cogency the many problems threatening the freedom of black people. Colonial theology did not critically reflect upon the need for change in the social and economic strata of society because that theology reflected the colonial experience. It was unable to speak from the Caribbean experience. In many ways colonial theology related the gospel to the horrors of oppression in such a way that the gospel became the justification for oppression. Theology became one method by which the ruling class ensured that black people were kept in bondage. Black people were taught that it was God's will that they remain slaves and, further, that God in his wisdom and providence had made them "to make a crop." Even where colonial theology did not explicitly advocate human bondage it was difficult for that theology to be the means of human freedom for the oppressed.

One of the emphases of colonial theology was on individual salvation. This emphasis ignored the unity of the community and became a religious tool to keep black people apart. In consequence, it destroyed the solidarity of the black family. Freedom was presented as a private thing, which one could gain at the expense of another's well-being. Precisely at this point, black religion, as articulated in obeah and myalism and later in Revivalism and Rastafarianism, provided an important corrective to colonial theology. Black religion sought to create a public space for human freedom as it drew upon native symbols and experiences that were intended to protect the black family from oppression.

Black religion began the process of decolonizing theology when it insisted that God was the freeing one, who was at work in history setting the victims free. The task of colonial theology in keeping intact the structures that alienate and oppress people is pinpointed in a sermon delivered by one of the leading nonconformist preachers of his day, the Reverend William Knibb. Knibb discovered that black people, under the leadership of Sam Sharp, were planning to take things into their own hands and overthrow the system of slavery. With his knowledge of colonial theology, Knibb sought to block the struggle for freedom by suggesting to the people that in the name of Jesus Christ they should be obedient to their masters and thereby please God.[1] But the strong wind of freedom blew messages of liberation among black people and they acted to change the world that was crushing them. Colonial theology also explicated a false eschatology, which was designed to postpone freedom to the afterlife, where the inequities and injustices of this life would be redressed. But black people in the expression of black religion pressed for historical freedom. Although they believed in eschatological freedom, they were impatient with any freedom that did not change the world in which they lived.

Caribbean theologian Idris Hamid sums up the ways in which colonial theology functioned both as a divisive tool and as an opium of the people. Colonial theology as

> an individualistic gospel set man against his brother. Each individual must see that his soul is saved. The concern for the community and the social health of society was largely ignored. It made man unconcerned for the needs of his neighbor. This militated against community mindedness. This individualism was further entrenched by sectarianism so that individuals and groups were set against each other. The concern for the neighbor was not to minister so much to his physical needs or material needs, as to his spiritual ones—get him to come to church, particularly your own denomination.[2]

Hamid goes on to call for the decolonization of theology and a new theological orientation in the Caribbean. The decolonization of theology would involve a new look at black history and provide some clues concerning the future toward which God calls black people. The insistence of colonial theology that faith be grounded in the beyond must be seen as one way in which the oppressors ensured that black people were denied their future. This approach to theology "defuturized" black people's past and sought to rob the people of their hope for freedom. To accept responsibility for one's future, according to Hamid, means going "far beyond responsibility for our political life and the search for new cultural forms. It involves the value system of a new society, the life style and values which are now inflicted on us through the printed word and mass media."[3]

It becomes apparent not only that Caribbean theology must talk about God and people in history, but that it must go beyond black religion in making a connection between Christian hope and freedom in history. In black religion the Rastafarians talked about a man-God who was black, and the Revivalists announced that God would arrive in Jamaica on the last day of April 1860. Alexander Bedward, the father of Revivalism in Jamaica, also promised to ascend to heaven on the last day of December 1920.

The fact that the man-God Haile Selassie died and the Revivalists were disappointed in their hope of the ascension and of God's arrival does indicate the need for a revision of some of these beliefs. One approach, I suggest, is the connection between hope and freedom in history. This connection would establish the first planks for a theology of freedom.

HOPE AND FREEDOM

One might argue that a more logical step would be from black religion to black theology rather than toward a theology of freedom. And although black theology as it is articulated in North America and South Africa is concerned with historical freedom, theological reflection in the Caribbean must guard against imports. From time to time, as Caribbean peoples seek to give theological substance to their understanding of historical freedom, it will be necessary to listen to other approaches. However, they must respect the particularity of each other's experience. The area in which I believe it would be most helpful to listen to the black American religious experience is that experience of faith as it was fashioned during slavery. This experience was one in which much exchange took place between Caribbean and black American peoples.

But someone may ask, Why not use the liberation theology of Latin America for the Caribbean? The counsel of Father Daniel P. Mulvey in "Liberation: Threat or Promise" should be heeded in this regard:

> . . . no matter its excellence, it [Latin American liberation theology] should not be seen as a "blue print" for the four corners of the world, and particularly the Caribbean. Gutiérrez is a Peruvian. He formally addresses himself to the problems and needs of Latin America. Too often in the past the Caribbean has been examined through European or North American glasses. There is no reason now to repeat past mistakes by viewing the Caribbean experience through Latin American lenses.[4]

One of the central concerns of theology in the Caribbean is social change. Father Mulvey fears that an imported theology would not be able to address this need with specificity and clarity. I would go further and suggest that, whereas liberation from socioeconomic and religious domination is a major task confronting Caribbean theology, liberation does not sum up the goal of theology. The goal of liberation is freedom. Liberation must aid people on the move into freedom. Freedom is not a state or a stage in the pilgrimage of black people and their God in history. Freedom is the vision of liberation. Hence it becomes the goal of any theology. This view seems to receive some credence in the recent assembly of the Caribbean Conference of Churches, which published the main addresses under the rubric, *Moving into Freedom.*[5] "It is for freedom that Christ has set us free" (Gal. 5:1).

However, there is a logical step from a consideration of black religion to an articulation of a theology of freedom, because black religion is black people's search in history for freedom. God was for black people the symbol of freedom. So, in the quest for a theology of freedom it becomes appropriate to ask about hope's relationship to freedom. The crucial question here is, Does hope set people free? This question is central for Christian theology because, if hope does not mean struggle for freedom in history, then it is the opium of the oppressed. For Christian theology to talk about hope without relating it to the struggle of the oppressed for freedom in history is for it tacitly to sanction the structures of oppression, which deprive the oppressed of their dignity.

To hope, then, is not merely to plan the future. Hope is more than the anticipation of freedom. It gives both form and content to human freedom. "The God who is always future is a God who does not become historical in terms of power but remains ahead attracting history to himself. . . ."[6]

The God who is revealed in Jesus Christ, although not limited to history, is present in history as savior, friend, and hope. Whenever the church forgets this it calls people to its ways and not to God's ways. Frantz Fanon in *The Wretched of the Earth* witnesses to this:

> The church in the colonies is the white people's church, the foreigner's church. She does not call the native to God's ways but to the ways of the white man, of the master, of the oppressor. And as we know, in this matter many are called but few chosen.[7]

Whenever the church fails to understand that the gospel of hope is the Good News of freedom, people are in danger of being treated as property. Then the future is projected as a continuation of the present. But hope that is grounded in the freedom of God becomes a critique of society as "the blind receive their sight and the lame walk, lepers are cleansed and the deaf hear, and the dead are raised up, and the poor have good news preached to them" (Matt. 11:5; cf. Lk. 4:18).

The Good News, then, is the summons to freedom where God reigns and victims are set free for freedom. Since black people regarded God as the source and symbol of freedom, we must now ask about the relationship between God and freedom.

GOD AND HUMAN FREEDOM

The failure of colonial theology to make a connection between God and human freedom allowed the early church in the Caribbean to condone human bondage. Whenever the church fails to make a connection between divine freedom and human freedom, it supports and gives its blessings to vicious structures of oppression in our world. This is often seen in the neutrality of a church's relationship to slums and shanty towns, which destroy black families and deny children their future. The inaction and unconcern of the church is due to its failure to discern God's liberating work in the world of human bondage.

At the second General Assembly of the Caribbean Conference of Churches, held in Guyana in 1977, the churches affirmed that God is the basis of human rights and freedom for black people. The Conference Report on Human Rights stated:

> In our journey of struggle for rights through self reliance, we resolve that our rights and nature have their foundation in our God and in his faithfulness. And while this might be a difficult principle to uphold in a characteristically cynical, scientific age, with not many dramatic examples of "the God who went before his people, winning their battles and demanding justice for them," there is a latent and indefatigable confidence that he sees our "condition" and "struggles" with us in our determination to change the present order.[8]

According to Caribbean Christians, God's freedom is for people. The deistic understanding of God is rejected here while God's commitment to the ordering of a new society is affirmed. This commitment to the building of a new community will see conflicts between the rich and the poor, the weak and the strong. But God's freedom ensures the determination to realize his justice in the world. With divine freedom as the basis of human freedom, Caribbean Christians affirm the kingdom of God as the kingdom of free humanity. The understanding that the kingdom of God has everything to do with the social and political responsibility of Christians in the world is upheld by Caribbean Christians. As Sehon Goodridge writes in "Christian Leadership in the Caribbean": "We are not saying that matter is here and spirit is elsewhere in some form of otherworldly state; . . . rather, we are categorically asserting that matter and spirit, body and spirit, are inextricably bound together. In a real sense matter must be viewed in relation to spirit, and spirit in relation to matter."[9]

Goodridge draws clearly the line between colonial theology and a theology of freedom. In colonial theology a connection was not made between saving the souls of black people and building an economy based on the brutalizing of black bodies. While the soul belonged to God, the body belonged to the master. Jamaican theologian Ashley Smith, in "Mission and Evangelism in an Age of Decolonization," points out that colonial theology used the concept of the kingdom of God to keep black people in bondage. The decolonization of theology would require "a form of spiritual rebirth and not merely an external political process. It connotes change in the relationship between peoples resulting from a transformation." For the dominated people, that would mean a consciousness of their own status as human beings, their strength to bring an end to their domination and subjugation; their ability to decide on the quality and direction of their future."[10] The call, then, is to affirm that to be Christian is to be free and that to be free for the kingdom of God is to be Christian. To be Christian is to be human, because the locus of freedom is the kingdom of God.

Talk concerning the freedom of God is a recognition that historical freedom is the center of the Christian faith. To respond to God's freedom is to recognize that historical freedom is a task which opens people up to divine freedom in which they encounter the transcendent in history. To participate in divine freedom is to offer to one the possibility to be free and to discover alternate ways to be human. When human freedom encounters divine freedom, the creation of a new humanity occurs. It is to become part of the realization that God's mission in the world is the creation of a new humanity. History then becomes the context in which this possibility of being human is realized.

To take responsibility for God's freedom in the world does not mean people become artisans of history merely in the sense of making "human life more human," but also in experiencing, in history, victory over the sin which separates one from another, from oneself, and from God. This reminds us that in Galatians 5:1—"For freedom Christ has set us free"— Paul was referring to freedom from sin, which represents a turning in upon oneself. According to Scripture, sin is the basic cause of injustice and oppression in the world. Sin understood as grounded in human will is not to negate the unjust structures in the world, but to recognize that behind those structures are personal and collective wills that reject God and neighbor. Precisely at this point the gospel says that the human response to God's freedom is to take responsibility for the ordering of the world. The oppressed who fail to ground their freedom to transform society in God's freedom become the victims of sin. They run the risk of forfeiting their ontological vocation to be free in history and their place in the kingdom of freedom and humanity.

GOD AND THE REVOLUTION

There is a revolution of sorts taking place in the Caribbean. The Cuban revolution kindled the political imagination of Caribbean peoples. An example of the impact Cuba is having in the Caribbean is illustrated in the relationship between Cuba and Jamaica, which are only ninety miles apart. The friendship between these two countries was reinforced in September 1973 when the Jamaican prime minister, Michael Manley, and Fidel Castro traveled together to Africa. In July 1975 Manley accepted the invitation of Castro to visit Cuba. Manley was accompanied by 160 fellow Jamaicans on his five-day visit. While in Cuba he received the nation's highest award, the José Martí National Award. On his return to Jamaica, Manley pledged to unite with Cuba to destroy imperialism and capitalism in Jamaica. He commented: "What we were able to see after 16 years of history is something amazing. No people in the world have such a feeling of happiness and contentment. . . . Cuba and Jamaica have both been destroyed by capitalism, but now we are building bridges to unite our two peoples."[11]

In December 1975, Manley gave a keynote address at the Fifth Assembly of the World Council of Churches in Nairobi, in which he alluded to many ways in which the capitalist, free-enterprise system had denuded Caribbean peoples of their dignity and had become the main source of oppression in Jamaica: the practice of capitalism has entrenched the master/slave relationship in the Caribbean and differs from early feudalism only in that the serfs could at least be sure that the air they breathed was clean. "Neither factory hand nor coal miner could be sure that even sunlight would form a significant part of his total waking experience." Manley continued:

> If capitalism was the engine that lifted man to new levels of economic and technological progress, it was equally the burial ground of his moral integrity. And as if the moral consequences of capitalism were not sufficiently disastrous for its supposed beneficiaries and all others who were caught in the system, it also proceeded historically in harness with that twin steed of ill fortune and oppression, imperialism. For imperialism was the means by which capitalism reproduced internationally all that it had done to human experience within national boundaries.[12]

In 1977 Fidel Castro paid his first visit to Jamaica, and affirmed the revolutionary struggles of these two peoples for freedom. During that visit he held a two-hour conversation with the Jamaican Council of Churches in which he pointed out that he was baptized by the church and that he did not see a conflict between religion and revolution. The problem in Cuba is not so much between the revolution and religious beliefs as between the revolution and a social class, Castro said, and he continued:

> The Church was served in Cuba by a clergy of foreign origin, most of the clergymen coming from Spain, it being the church of the rich people. That wasn't the same as in Latin America. In Latin America, in many countries, the Catholic Church exerts a broad influence on popular sectors. . . . In Cuba, unlike in France, for example, we had no priests who worked with the industrial workers or who went out into the fields and became one of them. That was not the situation that prevailed in Cuba. Suffice it to say that in Cuba there wasn't a single Catholic Church in the whole of the country-side. The Churches were mainly in the large cities.

Particular care was taken to ensure that during the Cuban revolution conflicts between the Castro government and religion were reduced to a minimum.

> . . . before the world, before our people, before other peoples, we took special care in never making the Cuban Revolution seem to be

the enemy of religion, because if that had happened we would have really been doing a service to the reactionaries, to the exploiters, not only in Cuba but above all in Latin America.[13]

The present government of Jamaica is committed to the death of the capitalist, free-enterprise system, which keeps intact the master/slave syndrome. A visit to Jamaica today reveals a dying capitalism and an emergent socialist form of government. The society Manley envisions for Jamaica is summed up in his remarks:

> . . . Socialism is love, . . . Socialism is Christianity in action. . . . Socialism is the Christian way of life in action. It is the philosophy that best gives expression to the Christian ideal of the equality of all God's children. It has as its foundation the Christian belief that all men and women must love their neighbours as themselves.[14]

Caribbean theologians have reflected on this new community that is coming to life in Jamaica, and in many Caribbean islands. Robert Cuthbert, for example, sees this modelled for us in Isaiah 65:20–28.

The creation of a community in the Caribbean where people will be celebrated for their presence was attested to by the Caribbean Ecumenical Consultation on Development in 1971. At this meeting 260 church and community leaders from twenty-five religious traditions and sixteen regions met to interpret God's will for the Caribbean. The resolutions produced at that consultation form the objectives for the agency called CADEC (Christian Action for Development in Caribbean). Some of the areas of need identified were:

> patterns of consumption less imitative of affluent societies and more suited to the needs and potentialities of the region. . . .

> an opportunity for a wider section of our people, especially those who now work the land, to become owners of it. . . .

> an education of persons which will make them conscious and critical of their situation and the situation of others, and enable them to act responsibly and morally in these situations. . . .[15]

The Caribbean Ecumenical Conference adopted a resolution expressing their hope that the new community in the Caribbean would reflect the following characteristics:

1. Maximum participation of people in the decision making process
2. Recognition of our assets—sea, air, and living patterns that are not oppressive

3. Housing, ecology and family life: emphasis should be on rural development (housing, roads, etc.), to prevent an uncontrolled growth of the city, bearing in mind that our economy must be largely based on agriculture.[16]*

The people of the Caribbean are experiencing history as revolutionary change. Because present capitalistic structures are not able to provide the context for the new Caribbean person to emerge, change is advocated in the structural basis of society: political, social, economic, moral, and religious. Freedom must mean action in history that will lead to the creation of a more just and humane society.

Caribbean theologian Sergio Arce Martínez, in "Christ and Liberation," points out that the marks of the socialist revolution are struggle and victory, more struggle and more victory. It is the presence of God in the struggle that guarantees the victory of freedom. Not only did God indicate his commitment to revolution in leading the children of Israel out of Egypt, but in Jesus of Nazareth he made it clear that freedom meant revolution. Arce says:

> Every attempt to liberate humanity from poverty, from oppression, from ignorance, from exploitation, as Jesus announced it in Nazareth naturally amounts to a revolution. The Revolution is destruction of the structure of slavery but it is more than that. It is re-creation of a person who frees himself or herself from vested interests to go in search of other, more genuinely human—that is more genuinely social—interests. . . . This is the historic movement which in the language of Luke is called the year of Grace of the Lord, remembering the year of Grace of the old covenant.[17]

In the struggle for freedom, the new Caribbean person will emerge. Freedom, in this struggle for a fuller humanity, will change the world in such a way that those who participate in the struggle will become worthy personal and social witnesses of God's freedom in the midst of an unjust world.

The gospel of the incarnation announces God's freedom as the instrument to break the power of human bondage and offers to all people the possibility to be free in history. This community—black Jamaica and all

---

* In order to give substance to the areas of need identified, the Caribbean Conference of Churches was founded in Jamaica, in November 1973, with an Inaugural Assembly. The purpose of the Conference of Churches is expressed in the opening words of its constitution: "We, as Christian people of the Caribbean, separated from each other by barriers of history, language, culture, class and distance, desire because of our common calling in Christ to join together in a regional fellowship of churches for inspiration, consultation and cooperative action" (*Caribbean Contact* 2, no. 9 [1974]: 7, 18).

oppressed peoples—must continue to assert, as the basis of its identity in history, that Jesus Christ *is*, therefore the oppressed *are free*.

NOTES

1. Trevor Munroe and Don Robotham, *Struggles of the Jamaican People* (Kingston: Worker's Liberation League, 1977), pp. 12–13.

2. Idris Hamid, *In Search of New Perspectives* (Bridgetown: Caribbean Ecumenical Consultation for Development, 1971), p. 6.

3. Ibid., p. 8.

4. Father Daniel P. Mulvey, S.J., "Liberation: Threat or Promise" in *Justice*, no. 10 (September 1973), p. 1.

5. Kortright Davis, ed., *Moving into Freedom* (Bridgetown: Cedar Press, 1977).

6. Rubem A. Alves, *A Theology of Human Hope* (New York/Cleveland: Corpus Books, 1971), p. 94.

7. Frantz Fanon, *The Wretched of the Earth* (New York: Grove Press, 1968), p. 42.

8. Caribbean Conference of Churches, Program Report on Human Rights (Guyana, November 16–23, 1977), p. 3.

9. Sehon Goodridge, "Christian Leadership in the Caribbean," in Davis, ed., *Moving into Freedom*, p. 7.

10. Ashley Smith, "Mission and Evangelism in an Age of Decolonization," in Idris Hamid, ed., *Out of the Depths* (San Fernando, Trinidad: Rahaman Printery, 1977), p. 115.

11. In Shepherd Bliss, "Setting Its Own Course," *Cuba Review* 7, no. 1, p. 19.

12. Michael Manley, *From the Shackles of Domination and Oppression*. Address Document No. 1, World Council of Churches, Fifth Assembly, Nairobi, Kenya, November 23–December 10, 1975, pp. 4–5.

13. See *Gramma*, no. 47 (official organ of the Central Committee of the Communist Party of Cuba), November 20, 1977, p. 6.

14. In Matthew Ryan, "Socialism—Jamaica Style," *Caribbean Contact* 1, David I. Mitchell, ed., no. 12 (March 1975): 5.

15. Robert Cuthbert, "Development and the Caribbean Christian," in David I. Mitchell, ed., *With Eyes Wide Open* (Bridgetown: CADEC, 1973), pp. 111–12. For a detailed account of the conference, see *Called to Be*, 2nd ed. (Bridgetown: CADEC, 1973), pp. 5–15.

16. Ibid., p. 113.

17. Sergio Arce Martínez, "Christ and Liberation," *Cuba Review* 5, no. 3, p. 405. For discussions of God in the Caribbean revolution, see Alice L. Hageman and Philip Wheaton, eds., *Religion in Cuba Today* (New York: Association Press, 1971); also David I. Mitchell, *New Mission for a New People* (New York: Friendship Press, 1977).

Index

Compiled by William E. Jerman, ASI

Other Orbis books . . .

THE MEANING OF MISSION

José Comblin

"This very readable book has made me think, and I feel it will be useful for anyone dealing with their Christian role of mission and evangelism." *New Review of Books and Religion*
ISBN 0-88344-304-X CIP   *Cloth $6.95*

THE GOSPEL OF PEACE AND JUSTICE

Catholic Social Teaching Since Pope John

Presented by Joseph Gremillion

"Especially valuable as a resource. The book brings together 22 documents containing the developing social teaching of the church from *Mater et Magistra* to Pope Paul's 1975 *Peace Day Message on Reconciliation*. I watched the intellectual excitement of students who used Gremillion's book in a justice and peace course I taught last summer, as they discovered a body of teaching on the issues they had defined as relevant. To read Gremillion's overview and prospectus, a meaty introductory essay of some 140 pages, is to be guided through the sea of social teaching by a remarkably adept navigator."

National Catholic Reporter

"An authoritative guide and study aid for concerned Catholics and others." *Library Journal*
ISBN 0-88344-165-9   *Cloth $15.95*
ISBN 0-88344-166-7   *Paper $8.95*

THEOLOGY IN THE AMERICAS

Papers of the 1975 Detroit Conference

Edited by Sergio Torres and John Eagleson

"A pathbreaking book from and about a pathbreaking theological conference, *Theology in the Americas* makes a major contribution to ecumenical theology, Christian social ethics and liberation movements in dialogue." *Fellowship*
ISBN 0-88344-479-8 CIP   *Cloth $12.95*
ISBN 0-88344-476-3   *Paper $5.95*

THE PRAYERS
OF AFRICAN RELIGION

John S. Mbiti

"We owe a debt of gratitude to Mbiti for this excellent anthology which so well illuminates African traditional religious life and illustrates so beautifully man as the one who prays." *Sisters Today*
ISBN 0-88344-394-5 CIP   *Cloth $7.95*

POLYGAMY RECONSIDERED

Eugene Hillman

"This is by all odds the most careful consideration of polygamy and the attitude of Christian Churches toward it which it has been my privilege to see." *Missiology*
ISBN 0-88344-391-0   *Cloth $15.00*
ISBN 0-88344-392-9   *Paper $7.95*

AFRICAN TRADITIONAL RELIGION

E. Bolaji Idowu

"A great work in the field and closely comparable to Mbiti's *African Religions and Philosophy*. It is worthwhile reading." *The Jurist*
ISBN 0-88344-005-9   *Cloth $6.95*

AFRICAN CULTURE
AND THE CHRISTIAN CHURCH

Aylward Shorter

"An introduction to social and pastoral anthropology, written in Africa for the African Christian Churches." *Western Catholic Reporter*
ISBN 0-88344-004-0   *Paper $6.50*

TANZANIA AND NYERERE

William R. Duggan & John R. Civille

"Sympathetic survey of Tanzania's attempt to develop economically on an independent path." *Journal of World Affairs*
ISBN 0-88344-475-5 CIP   *Cloth $10.95*

MARX AND THE BIBLE

José Miranda

"An inescapable book which raises more questions than it answers, which will satisfy few of us, but will not let us rest easily again. It is an attempt to utilize the best tradition of Scripture scholarship to understand the text when it is set in a context of human need and misery."

Walter Brueggemann, in Interpretation

ISBN 0-88344-306-6   *Cloth $8.95*
ISBN 0-88344-307-4   *Paper $4.95*

BEING AND THE MESSIAH

The Message of Saint John

José Miranda

"This book could become the catalyst of a new debate on the Fourth Gospel. Johannine scholarship will hotly debate the 'terrifyingly revolutionary thesis that this world of contempt and oppression can be changed into a world of complete selflessness and unrestricted mutual assistance.' Cast in the framework of an analysis of contemporary philosophy, the volume will prove a classic of Latin American theology." *Frederick Herzog, Duke University Divinity School*

ISBN 0-88344-027-X CIP   *Cloth $8.95*
ISBN 0-88344-028-8   *Paper $4.95*

THE GOSPEL IN SOLENTINAME

Ernesto Cardenal

"Upon reading this book, I want to do so many things—burn all my other books which at best seem like hay, soggy with mildew. I now know who (not what) is the church and how to celebrate church in the eucharist. The dialogues are intense, profound, radical. *The Gospel in Solentiname* calls us home."

Carroll Stuhlmueller, National Catholic Reporter

ISBN 0-88344-168-3   *Vol. 1 Cloth $6.95*
ISBN 0-88344-170-5   *Vol. 1 Paper $4.95*
ISBN 0-88344-167-5   *Vol. 2 Cloth $6.95*

LOVE AND STRUGGLE
IN MAO'S THOUGHT

Raymond L. Whitehead

"Mao's thoughts have forced Whitehead to reassess his own philosophy and to find himself more fully as a Christian. His well documented and meticulously expounded philosophy of Mao's love and struggle-thought might do as much for many a searching reader." *Prairie Messenger*

ISBN 0-88344-289-2 CIP   *Cloth $8.95*
ISBN 0-88344-290-6   *Paper $3.95*

WATERBUFFALO THEOLOGY

Kosuke Koyama

"This book with its vivid metaphors, fresh imagination and creative symbolism is a 'must' for anyone desiring to gain a glimpse into the Asian mind." *Evangelical Missions Quarterly*

ISBN 0-88344-702-9   *Paper $4.95*

ASIAN VOICES
IN CHRISTIAN THEOLOGY

Edited by Gerald H. Anderson

"A basic sourcebook for anyone interested in the state of Protestant theology in Asia today. I am aware of no other book in English that treats this matter more completely." *National Catholic Reporter*

ISBN 0-88344-017-2   *Cloth $15.00*
ISBN 0-88344-016-4   *Paper $7.95*

FAREWELL TO INNOCENCE

Allan Boesak

"This is an extremely helpful book. The treatment of the themes of power, liberation, and reconciliation is precise, original, and Biblically-rooted. Dr. Boesak has done much to advance the discussion, and no one who is interested in these matters can afford to ignore his important contribution." *Richard J. Mouw, Calvin College*

ISBN 0-88344-130-6 CIP   *Cloth $4.95*